Family Violence in India

Family Violence in India

Edited by

Dr. Subhash Chandra Singh
Head & Dean, Faculty of Law
M. G. Kashi Vidyapith, Varanasi, (U.P.)

SERIALS PUBLICATIONS
NEW DELHI (INDIA)

First Published - 2010

ISBN: 978-81-8387-394-9

Published by

SERIALS PUBLICATIONS
4830/24, Prahlad Street, Ansari Road
Darya Ganj, New Delhi-110002 (India)
Phone : 23245225 Fax : 91-11-23272135
E-mail: serials@sify.com

Contens

Preface

Domestic Violence towards women, girls is a world wide phemonon of concern. Domestic violence is not imparted only physically but emotionally, psychologically, internal partner violence, sexual abuse, intimidating, stalking, passive covert abuse, abuse of girl child, prostitution, etc. Domestic violence is a serious human rights violation. It is assumed that every women is a victim of domestic violence only, the form and intensity differs, inspite of the fact that plethora of laws, legislations, acts are available to protect the women. In these days of terror and terrorism women's rights are civil, social, cultural political. In addition to this, women's rights to health, education, property have to be provided. We have to change the concept that women are slaves to men.

The book covers Domestic Violence through various concepts as discussed in these valuable, scholarly research studies. The research papers are- Domestic Violence against men: a neglected social aspect, Domestic Violence: An assessment of global scenario, Status of women: A critical approach with reference to Human Rights, Women under Labour Laws, Study of Issues and Violence on Dual Role of working women in Chennai City, Domestic Violence in India: A Milestone in Protection of Women, Domestic Violence: Against Women in India, Elder Abuse and Factors, Violence against women with special reference to dowry deaths in India and lastly Domestic Violence in India.

Gurpreet Pannu, Reader in the Department of Law, Punjabi University Patiala, has discussed domestic violence against men-a neglected social aspect. This article is quite different to other articles on domestic violence. Domestic Violence is being discussed in present day parlance viz only towards women, girls, children. This highlights very important social aspect which has been neglected so far. Domestic violence is a serious human right violation. It is widely prevailing assumption that women are always the victims and men are always the perpetrators. Since ancient times women complained of being abused and subjugated by men and law has taken these allegations very seriously. But now it is male fraternity who claim to be at the receiving end.

Research has shown that only women are not the victims of domestic violence but husbands also face domestic violence in one way or the other. The article besides defining domestic violence, discusses issue of domestic violence against men which is totally neglected issue in the society. It cites statistics to prove the point that domestic violence and abuse is also met by men. In US, physically abused men are sixth of total patients admitted to hospitals reporting domestic violence as cause of their injuries. A survey in England showed that men and women are equally violent (4.2% men and 4.2% women do the crime of domestic violence) 30% men had been attacked while asleep, 25% men had been kicked in the genitals. A study conducted by two NGOs, on domestic violence against men showed that Indian women are more abusive and dominating. The survey cites tables of violence done towards men by women. Domestic violence against men go unrecognized and cases remain unreported. The article also streamlines the causes of domestic violence against men. Social norms, misuse of existing Anti-Dowry Laws by women, misuse of Protection of Women from Domestic Violence Act, alcohol abuse, dependency of men on women, psychological disorder etc. It also examines critically examines the Domestic Violence Act and points out discrepancies which encourage domestic violence against men.

Duraipandi Mavoothu, Reader School of Management Study, Cochin University, Cochin, in his article entitled, ' Domestic Violence: An assessment of Global Scenario' Catch hold of this problem globally. Domestic Violence which has so far been a minor problem has assumed the position of serious human right violation and public health problem. Gender-Specific forms of abuse comprises, aggression against and exploitation of women, because they are women. Many of these sex-specific violations are sexual or reproduction related including rape, sexual murder, battery, honor killing, dowry burnings, female genital mutilation (FGM), prostitution, forced abortions, sterilization and sexual violations of any kind. Various studies conducted on the subject have been viewed and results printed. A study findings show that women in Bangladesh, Morocco, and Uganda experience multiple and severe forms of violence by an intimate partner, yet a majority of them do not seek help. Domestic Violence and Rapes continue to rise in Malaysia, despite efforts. The article defined domestic violence in a lucid and comprehensive manner citing Indian and American views shape of laws. In addition, forms of domestic violence, types of domestic violence, causes of domestic violence find proper treatment. It has been observed that as many as 275 million children worldwide become caught in the cross-fire of domestic violence. Violence against Children involves physical and psychological abuse and injury and neglect. Children who exposed to domestic violence suffer symptoms of positive-traumic stress disorder. UN Study on violence against children represents a crucial step towards unmasking the issue of violence against children including abuses. The article presents guiding principles of the Report of Independent Experts for the UN Study on violence against children. Current global problems have also been highlighted against domestic violence. Also discuss health care issues in connection with domestic violence. Suggestions on assessment of global scenario on domestic violence are given by the author - as income equilibrium, utility outside of the marriage, new laws and funding, responsible fatherhood, climate change and psychology, political will, awareness of physicians, etc.

ND Gowda and Maruthi TR of Law Faculties in Karnataka, critically examine the status of women with reference to human rights. Human Rights, the most fundamental of all rights are the rights of people. The concept of Women's human rights owes its use to the fact that it is simultaneously prosaic and revolutionary on one hand, the idea of women's human rights make sense. Women's Human Rights are a revolutionary notion. UN Declaration for Women (1976-85), Women from many geographical, racial, religious, cultural and class background took up organizing to improve the status of women. UN sponsored women's Conferences, Universal Declaration of Human Rights states, 'No one shall be subject to torture or to cruel, inhuman or degrading treatment or punishment. The article defines and discusses human rights framework to women, UN Declaration against Violation against women passed by the General Assembly affirmed that in case of conflict between women human rights and cultural or religious practices, the human rights of women must prevail. UN has passed several conventions on women's rights. The study discusses elaborately all the relevant world conventions related women's rights, elimination of discrimination etc.

Women Under Labour Law, by Maruthi, TR, University Mysore, Karnataka, has studied the subject in detailed lucid manner. The predominant and pervading patriarchal system created disadvantages for women in every sphere and at all the stages of life. In reality, there is no doubt, that women all over the world have made tremendous progress. Social status has been improved, still the problems pertaining to their health, employment, social equality, social discrimination, violence, atrocity, remains the same. Women's rights to equality with men is accepted and promoted in international development organizations and in the development plans and policies of may developing countries. The paper deeply and seriously examines all the relevant Acts, eg. Factores Act, Mines Act, Plantation Labour Act etc. The restrictions under these acts have also been removed. Labour Legislations in all applicable spheres must be vigorously implemented. Women must fight back for their participation and respond to the demands of progress in order to improve women's status. The government has passed stringent laws for harassment of women at work place. Section 509 of IPC prescribes punishment for a ward, gesture, or act intended to outrage the industry of women. The central and state governments have enacted laws to benefit women, as Maternity Benefits, Medical Bonus, Mines Maternity Benefit Act, 1951. In order to improve women's position in industry several other measures have been made. To improve women's lot further, Regional and International instruments of International Labor Law, have been enacted as NAFTA, CARICOM, SADC and COMESA. UN General Assembly has also adopted a number of legally binding conventions concerning labor matters. Therefore we find positive and effective contribution of legislation in protecting the interest of women workers through legislative processes. The present penal provisions in labour legislation are instrument to deter the employer.

Prof. R. Balasubramanian, has made study of issues and violence in dual role of working women in Chennai City (TN). Women's access to jobs may onece have been a forbidden issue, but in today's highly competitive and tough economic environment, job is now an essential thing for most women. Working women perform dual role to sustain the family. The dual role of working women today is a necessary characteristics of modern society. Many studies have identified education, work participation, experience, cadre of job and exposure to outside living conditions as determinants for women economic status. Economic, Social, political and holistic empowerment of women is a must to women emancipation and progress in the society.

Rattan Singh and Mehal Ahuja, have comprehensively discussed domestic violence in India and a milestone achieved by India in the Protection of Women. Violence against women and girls is the most pervasive human right violation in the world today. We live in a democratic society where women constitute nearly one-half of the population. From times immemorial, a women has not only denied justice, equality, liberty, but she has also been socially, economically, physically, psychologically, emotionally as well as sexually exploited at home, in office, and everywhere and has been forced to lead an immoral and destitute life. Parliament has enacted a law namely, 'The Protection of Women from Domestic Violence Act, 2005'. Violence against women is also protected in several other laws which have been discussed elaborately. Some of these are - Indian evidence Act, Muslim Women (Protection of Rights on Divorce), Indecent Representation of Women (Prohibition) Act, 1986, Dowry Prohibition Act, 1961, Criminal Procedure Code, 1973, Hindu Marriage Act, Hindu Adoption and Maintenance Act, 1956, Hindu Succession Act, 1956, Family Courts Act, CEDAW, Protection of Women under Domestic Violence Act, (PWDVA) etc. The study also discusses Domestic Violence in other countries like Malaysia, Bulgaria, Brazil, Brunei, Bangladesh, Pakistan. The various provisions of Indian Constitution, Laws, Acts, Ruels, Commission, Conventions and Declarations are there and the problems of women for Domestic Violence Act, 2005, also has been enacted to prohibit violence against women to provide her equal status to men but still these exists the wide gaps.

The other articles in the volume also streamline constitutional provisions, laws, acts, rules, commissions related domestic violations against women in India. These also deal with elderly abuse etc.

It is also hoped that these information and comprehensive articles on Domestic Violence are to great value to sociologists, research scholars in the field of sociology, constitutional laws and all the libraries and information centers. These articles also make a useful study to gain Indian position as well as position of other countries in relation to domestic violence towards women, their socio-economic, political status and relevant provisions of laws which positively favour women against violence, at home and at the working place.

Dr. Subhash Chandra Singh

Domestic Violence Against Men– A Neglected Social Aspect

GURPREET PANNU*

INTRODUCTION

DOMESTIC violence is a serious human rights violation. It is widely prevailing assumption that women are always the victims and men are always perpetrators. Women have always complained of being oppressed and beaten by men with the approval of societies dominated by men. Since the ancient times women complained of being abused and subjugated by men and law has taken these social allegations very seriously. But now it is male fraternity, who claim to be at receiving end. Research has shown that only women are not the victims of domestic violence, but husbands also face domestic violence in one way or other.

The assumption that every woman is victim of domestic violence, only the form and intensity differs, and men are the victimizers is the reason for enforcing plethora of laws protecting the women in the family and society. This is the reason for spending millions of rupees of public money on women's groups and there is none to help male. Men also know that there is little support they will receive if they tell others that they were abused by their wives or girlfriends, and more likely to be ridiculed than taken seriously. Men are expected to take abuse "like a man" and not complain.

There is a social message which tells us that woman is being victimized by the male dominating society for centuries and it is not objectionable if a woman hits man. It is a sign of awakening up of women and is portrayed as a justified act, sometimes even a humour. Rather than thinking that a woman hitting a man is violence, we are led to think, "he must have done something wrong to her to deserve being hit." This double standard also contributes to the under

* *Reader, Department of Law, Punjabi University, Patiala.*

reporting of domestic violence against man. We do not consider is as a crime if a woman hits a man.

When a man, who is victim of domestic violence, tries to tell his problems of marriage and family, no one gets ready to listen, instead they laugh at him. Many men are ashamed to talk about that they are beaten by wife and her family, because of Indian mentality. This paper is an attempt to discuss the issue of domestic violence against men, which is totally neglected issue in our society. The scope of present paper is to discuss the meaning of domestic violence, factors responsible for such violence and legal tackling of this problem.

MEANING OF DOMESTIC VIOLENCE

There is no universally accepted definition of domestic violence. Some human rights activists prefer a broad based definition which includes "structural violence" such as poverty and unequal access to health and education. Others have argued for a more limited definition in order no to lose the actual descriptive power of the term. In any case the need to develop specific operational definitions has been acknowledged so that research and monitoring can become more specific and have greater cross-cultural applicability.[1]

In United States of America domestic violence means, "Domestic violence is a pattern of abusive behaviour in any relationship that is used by one partner to gain or maintain power and control over another intimate partner."[2]

The Children and Family Courts Advisory and Support Service in United Kingdom in its "Domestic Violence Policy" uses domestic violence to refer to a range of violence and abusive behaviour and defines it as "Patterns of behaviour characterized by the misuse of power and control by one person over another who are or have been in an intimate relationship. It can occur in mixed gender relationship and same gender relationships and has profounded consequences for the lives of children, individuals, families and communities. It can be physical, sexual, emotional or psychological. It may include intimidation, harassment, damage to property, threats and financial abuse."

The New York State coalition defines domestic violence as "abusive behaviour-emotional, psychological, physical or sexual - that one person in an intimate relationship uses in order to control the other. It takes many different forms and includes behaviours such as threats, name - calling, preventing contact with family or friends, withholding money, actual or threatened physical harm and sexual assault. Stalking can also be a form of domestic violence."

Domestic violence is also known as domestic abuse or spousal abuse. It often refers to violence between spouses but can also include cohabitants and non-married intimate partner. It includes number of dimensions:

(a) *Mode:* Physical, psychological, verbal and social.

(b) *Frequency:* On/of occasional and chronic.

(c) *Severity:* In terms of both psychological or physical harm and need for treatment.

(d) *Transitory or permanent injury:* Mild, moderate, severe and upto homicide.

An important component of domestic violence often ignored is the realm of passive abuse leading to violence. Passive abuse is covert, subtle and veiled. This includes victimization, procrastination, forgetfulness, ambiguity, neglect, spiritual and intellectual abuse. Domestic violence includes slapping, hitting, throwing objects, forcing or slamming a door or striking the other person with a weapon.[3] A significant number of men are very sensitive to emotional and psychological issues and in some cases, humiliating a man emotionally in front of other men can be more devastating than physical violence. Some professionals have observed that mental and emotional abuse can be an area where women are much more 'brutal' than man. Men on the other hand are quicker to resort to physical abuse and they are more capable of physical assaults that are more brutal-even deadly[4]. Men are emotionally abused much more than women in the family and scars of emotional violence are often more painful than physical abuse.[5]

There are different modes of violence against men in the family like when he comes home to be tired from work, wife starts to grumble. Most of Indian wives are housewives, when husband comes back from work, they deliberately delay the serving of food on time and some husbands prepare food for themselves. For some women sex is a bargaining tool to get things done from husband. Even he is not having sex he can be charged with rape, if not charged with impotent. Many wives force their husbands to send out his parents to orphanage or old age home and many women do not look after parents-in-law. Most of the women are verbally abusive and they know how to insult men, even his old aged parents in front of him or *vise versa*.

STATISTICS ABOUT DOMESTIC VIOLENCE AND ABUSE AGAINST MEN

Very little is known about the actual number of men who are in a domestic relationship in which they are abused and treated violently by women. Very few cases are reported to police and authorities, so the data is limited.

United States of America

In a special report on violence related injuries by US Department of Justice[6], hospital emergency room visits pertaining of domestic violence indicated that physically abused men represent just are sixth of the total patients admitted in hospital reporting domestic violence as the cause of their injuries.

Recent available data[7] shows that:

- In U.S.A. 3.2 million men are victims of assault and abuse (like pushing, grabbing, showing slapping and hitting) per year, though many are more serious and end in homicide.
- Approximately 8,00,000 men (3.2%) are raped or physically assaulted by their partner per year.
- At least 3,71,000 men are stalked annually.
- 3% of fatal violence against men stems from domestic victims.
- Approximately 22% of men have experienced physical, sexual or psychological intimate partner violence during their life.
- In 2002, 24% of U.S. homicides that were as a result of Intimate Partner violence were men.
- 25,473 Washington men a year face domestic abuse.[9]
- 15% of intimate partner victim were men.
- Every 37.8 seconds, some where in America a man is battered.
- Every 20.6 minutes another man in Washington is battered.

Position in England

In 1999 as survey conducted in England has been published by the government relating to domestic violence.[10] It was the biggest ever carried out anywhere in the world and involved more than 10,000 men and women. It was called study 191 and it stated, quite categorically, that 4.2% of men and 4.2% of women perpetuate the crime of domestic violence. In other words, they had discovered that men and women are quite equally violent.[11]

A dispatches programme broadcast in the England on 7th January 1999 reported on the experiences of 100 male victims of domestic violence and found that:

- 30% had been attacked while asleep;
- 25% had been kicked in the genitals;
- 25% of male victims had themselves been arrested after seeking police help; and 89% felt that the police had not taken their complaints seriously;
- Only 7% of females assailants had been arrested and none was subsequently charged.

There are only two refuges for men, victims of domestic violence. In England, one opened in December 2003 and another, which is only one exclusively for men, in January 2004.

Indian Scenario

Though Indian society is considered to be male dominated and conservative society, by a survey[12] has found that large number of Indian husbands say that they have faced domestic violence in one form or the other during married life.

The study conducted by two non government organizations–Save Family Foundation and My Nation–on domestic violence against men between March 2005 to September 2007, looked at four types of domestic violence–physical, emotional, economic and sexual. In a sample survey of 1650 urban men, almost 98% of respondents said that they had suffered violence under one or the other of these heads more than once.

- Economic abuse was found to be the most common complaint with 32.79% saying they had faced it at least once in their married life.
- Emotional abuse 22.18%
- Physical abuse 25.21%
- Sexual abuse 17.70%
- Approximately 43% of husbands said they contemplated suicide due to humiliation, harassment and frustration and 14% accepted that they had wanted to kill the woman and her family members for instigating her.

This study concluded that Indian women are most abusive and dominating:

Domestic Violence against Indian Men

In the year 2007, 57,593 married men committed suicide compared to 30,064 married woman.[13] Every 8 minutes one Indian man ends life and chances are 200% higher after marriage.[14] It is interesting to note that the probability of violence increase significantly with the duration of marriage. Nagging, grumbling, taunting, name calling, refusing food, denying sexual intercourse, snatching salary, throwing objects, scratching with nails and biting, threats of suicide are some of the common forms of domestic violence.

Table 1
Type of Violence Reported

India	*People Interview*	*Physical Violence*	*Verbal/ Emotional Violence*	*Economic Violence*	*Sexual Abuse*	*No Violence*	*Total*
Total	1650	416 25.21%	368 22.18%	541 32.79%	292 17.70%	33 2.00%	1650

Table 2
Agewise

India	*People Interview*	*15-25 years*	*26-35 years*	*35-45 years*	*45 and above*	*Total*
Total	1650	92 5.58%	1105 66.97%	385 23.33%	68 4.12%	1650

Table 3
Profession of People

	People Interview	*Marketing*	*Doctor/ Engg.*	*Self Employed*	*Govt. Job*	*Unemployed*	*Total*
Total	1650	326 19.76%	635 38.48%	399 24.18%	262 15.88%	28 1.70%	1650

REASONS RESPONSIBLE FOR UNDER REPORTING OF CASES OF DOMESTIC VIOLENCE AGAINST MEN

Domestic violence against men goes unrecognized and cases remain unreported due to following reasons:

- The incidence of domestic violence against men seems to be so low that it is hard to get reliable estimate about the number of cases.
- The idea that men could be victims of domestic abuse and violence is still unthinkable in our society that majority of people do not believe it. So the victim does not dare to approach to the police and authorities to report such an incident.
- In majority of cases, the actual physical damage inflicted by men is much greater than the actual physical harm inflicted by women. The impact of domestic violence is less apparent and less likely to come to the attention of others.
- Even if a man dares to report an incident of domestic violence and abuse, people are so astonished, so the victim thinks that no body would believe him and the victim drops the idea.
- Our society and system has always responded to domestic violence against women. All the efforts have been made to stop abuse against women. There is negligible investment in resources and efforts to address the issues of domestic violence against male fraternity.
- Since long only women have been encouraged to raise voice against domestic violence and to report such case to authorities. Actually nothing has been done to encourage men to report such abuse.

CAUSES FOR DOMESTIC VIOLENCE AGAINST MEN

Our society and culture has always portrayed all women as victims of male dominated society. It is an accepted fact that the society has always revolved around the importance of women and we have always been deceived by saying, "men in the society victimize women". Men have always respected women in the family but let people know that men are abusing women. Fabricate and false cases are registered against men by the wives. Following causes are responsible for domestic violence against men:

Social Norms: Our society has always depicted man as very strong and care taker of the family and wife. This assumption prevails that girl needs money, protection etc., but we fail to understand that there has been a serious role reversal of the perpetrator of violence and victim of violence, wherein the victim being hailed as a criminal, is forced to compensate the tormentor, being hailed as a victim. Men also feel great that they are protecting a woman. Our society shows man as a protector of woman throughout her life. Woman is always shown as weaker sex. It looks highly delirious for a man to survive in a society suffering from double standard. Our social structure and norms are responsible that why we are never ready to believe that a man can also be victim of domestic violence.

Misuse of existing anti-dowry laws by women: There are many legislations enacted to protect women from becoming victims of dowry greed and to punish those who torture and even kill brides for dowry. These laws are to protect and empower the women. But now these laws are being misused. There are a number of husbands and in-laws getting thrown into slammer on the basis of more accusation of torture of dowry and a complaint under section 498-A of Indian Penal Code. The misuse of laws is termed as 'legal terrorism'. These laws are for misuse and social malaise.

As per the Times Online Polls conducted in 2007 on whether anti-dowry laws in India are biased against the men folk, the result was that 69% agree with it and 27% disagree and response of 4% voters was that they cannot say that these laws are biased or not.[15] Another survey conducted by Orissa's State Women Commission found that women are increasingly using dowry related laws like section 498-A of Indian Penal Code and Domestic Violence Act to harass husbands and to settle scores with them.

Thus instead of protecting the women, these laws are terrorizing and harassing the men folk in our society.

Misuse of Protection of Women from Domestic Violence Act: The implementation of Domestic Violence Act, 2005 has been referred by critics as anti-males, anti-marriage and anti-family. Keeping in mind the agenda of women-empowerment and protection, the overzealous government has trampled upon the fundamental right of men. It an acknowledged fact that domestic violence is a reality and husbands and their families perpetrate violence, but more than often husbands are at receiving end and brutalized by unruly women and their parents. It hurts many innocent males and their helpless old aged parents, who are put behind bars on false complaints.[16]

Many times false complaints are filed against politicians, higher officers, etc. though courts drop such false charges, but any action can not be taken against those who had misused the Domestic Violence Act.

Alcohol Abuse: Alcohol abuse is a major cause and trigger in domestic violence. People who are intoxicated have less impulse control, are easily frustrated, have greater misunderstandings and generally prove to resort to violence as a solution to problems. Women who are addicted are less adjustable in family. Such type of people cannot solve the problems in life they blame others for their problems and ultimately resort to violence. Women who abuse men are frequently alcoholics.

Dependency of Men on Women: Sometimes men are mentally and emotionally weak and they become dependent on wives. Such women exploit the weakness of men. Such women are in a dominating position and they try to show that they are more smarter, stronger and more powerful than men. The abused victim man is mentally, emotionally or financially dependent on the abusive woman. The idea of leaving the relationship creates significant feelings of insecurity, depression and anxiety. Such women try to exploit the weak men.

Psychological Disorders: Sometimes there are psychological problems, primarily personality disorders, in which women are characteristically abusive and violent towards men. Borderline Personality disorder is a diagnosis that is found almost exclusively with women. Approximately 1 to 2 percent of all women have a Borderline Personality disorder. At least 50% of all domestic abuse and violence against men is associated with such disorder. This disorder is also associated with suicidal behaviour, sever mood swings, lying, sexual problems and alcohol abuse.[17]

Unrealistic expectations, assumption and conclusion: Another reason for domestic violence against men is that the women who are abusive towards men usually have unrealistic demands of man. These women will typically experience repeated episodes of depression, anxiety, frustration and irritability which they attribute to a man's behavour. In fact, their mental and emotional state is the result of their own insecurities, emotional problems, trauma during childhood. Such women blame the men rather than admit their problems and to take responsibility of their own. They refuse to take treatment and may even insist the man to take treatment. Instead to helping themselves, they blame others and believe that husband should do something to feel them better and cure. Sometimes such women medicate their emotions with alcohol. Such women become frustrate and assume that their husbands are responsible for it.

PROTECTION OF WOMEN FROM DOMESTIC VIOLENCE ACT, 2005 VIS-À-VIS FUNDAMENTAL RIGHTS OF MEN

Under International law as well as national law right to equality and equal protection of law is available to men and woman. Some of special laws are enacted for the protection and upliftment of women in the society. No one can raise objection to ongoing efforts for empowerment and upliftment of women, but the way men and their rights have been set aside with a morbid concentration on women and their exaggerated rights, shows lack of gender neutral laws and against the right to equality before the law.[18]

On 26th October, 2006 Central Government enforced Protection of Women from Domestic Violence Act, 2005.[19] If we go through the provisions of this Act, there are certain provisions, which are enough to exploit the men by the women. Following provisions are against the interests and rights of men:

- It is presumed that only woman can be victim of domestic violence and she is referred as 'aggrieved' and husband is the 'respondent'. It presumes that in all the cases woman is victim and man is the abuser.
- Act provides that threat of abuse or actual abuse includes - physical, verbal, emotional or economic.[20]
- Act provides that information regarding an act or acts of domestic violence does not necessarily have to be lodged by the aggrieved party but by any person, who has reason to believe that such an act has been committed. It means that any relative, neighbour, social worker can take initiative on behalf of the victim.[21]
- Section 2 (a) includes live-in-relationship or sexual partner. Act legitimizes the extra-marital relations.
- Preventing one's wife from taking up a job or forcing her to leave job are also under the preview of the Act.
- Act allows magistrate to protect that woman from acts of violence or even "acts that are likely to take place" in future and can prohibit the respondent (man) from dispossessing the aggrieved person (woman) or in any other manner disturbing her possession, entering the woman's place of work or any other place that the abused woman frequents.[22]
- Another loophole in the existing law is that under the sole testimony of the aggrieved person, the court may conclude that offence has been committed by accused.[23] It means that even on false statement of woman, she is empowered to punish men. This is enough dangerous for men folk.
- The present Act has provided another tool to women in the form of "right to residence".[24] It means that wife can kick out the husband from matrimonial house, whenever she wants.

The above provisions of the present Act are enough to harass the men. People are misusing these provisions, for example the case, where Wipro Chairman was dragged to court under Domestic Violence Act was a clear cut case of misuse.[25] The Sting operation revealed that false medical certificate from government hospital doctors are issued to a women for rupees ten thousands to send husband behind bars and file false case of wife beating under section 498-A IPC and Domestic Violence Act.[26]

In *Save the Husband Foundation v. Union of India*,[27] a non-government organization challenged the constitutional validity of Protection of Women from Domestic Violence Act, 2005 on the following grounds:

(a) The nature of the Act is such that it hampers the normal day-to-day life of every 'domestic relationship' as defined in the Act will always hang over his head.

(b) The definition of domestic violence under section 3(d) includes sexual, verbal, emotional and economic abuse and cryptically defined, is vague and too wide and it can hamper day-to-day life of respondent. Thus the definition violates Articles 14, 19(1)(a) and 21 of Constitution of India.

(c) The acts, commission or omission of which the respondent is sought to be made liable under section 3 of the Act are devoid of any suffix relating to *mens rea*. The absence of terms such as 'intentionally, having knowledge or reason to believe' as an ingredient of the act is conspicuous. Thus the Act may be misused to include penalizing the respondent under the Act for those acts which were unintentional, accidental or otherwise arising out of bonafide mistake. This is violative of Article 21 and 14 of Constitution of India.

(d) The definition of 'domestic relationship' in section 2(f) of the Act includes the terms 'relationship in the nature of marriage' is not defined. India being a multifarious society the incidents, implications, interpretation of term would be varied and thus the term is vague and incapable of precise meaning. Thus the vagueness of the above term violates Article 14 of Constitution of India.

(e) The proviso to section 2(q) of the Act provides a remedy to a female living in a 'relationship in the nature of marriage'. The remedy is given to a person who is not a wife. The sweeping remedies envisaged by this Act should not provide any protection to such a woman especially when the other categories to which protection is granted are relationships by consanguinity, and marriage. Unequal are treated equally and if this position exists it violates Article 14 of Indian Constitution.

(f) The remedy envisaged under the Act is also available against a relative of the husband or male partner under the proviso to section 2 (q) of the Act. The Act is silent as to who constitutes 'a relative' for this purpose of the Act. The misuse of this Act may manifest itself as the husband/male partner may be held liable for the acts of his 'relatives'. The above inclusion of the term without proper explanation is violative to Article 14 and 21 of Constitution.

(g) The protection order envisaged under section 18(e) of the Act is violative of Article 19(1)(g) of Constitution of India as it seeks to prohibit the respondent from operating bank locker or accounts held singly by him. In a given case this may amount to violating Article 21 of Constitution as respondent's subsistence might be prejudiced.

(h) The nature of the relief envisaged under section 20 (1)(d) relating to maintenance is in addition to the remedy under section 125 of Code of Criminal Procedure, 1973. This amounts to vexing the respondent twice and is thus violative of the Constitution.

Thus the Act not only gives powers without taking any responsibility to women but also takes away all the rights of men. There is ample chance to misuse because there is no clause of punishment if misused, like dowry law.

In order to raise voice against misuse of Domestic Violence Act, Save Family Foundation, Delhi and Parivas Raksha Samiti, Chandigarh held protest against the misuse of women protection laws and demand gender neutrality of Domestic Violence Act on 3rd Anniversary of Domestic Violence Act on October 25, 2009 at Jantar Mantar, New Delhi and celebrated this day as 'Black Day'. The decision was taken to fight against misuse of women protection laws and conspiracy to destroy the family system of India. Slogan was raised to prevent India from becoming a Father less society. Decision was taken to celebrate month of October as 'Domestic Violence Against Men Awareness Month'.[28]

CONCLUSION AND SUGGESTIONS

The institution of family is the base of our society. Due to many reasons institution of family and its unity is under threat in our country. Women protective laws were enforced to empower and uplift the women in society, but these laws have been misused by few of people and due to this we have been unable to empower the women, but we are at the verge of destroying the sacred institution of marriage. Unless husband and wife are not loyal and bring immense good will and sacrifice to bear upon their marital fortunes, their situation is desperate. The need is for laws which ensure women their rightful, honourable place and at the same time we can not forget and ignore the rights of men. These laws are not to show disgrace and humiliation to male fraternity of our society. It has headed our society towards crisis, unrest and breakages of homes causing damage to the social fabric.

Domestic violence is not a gender based issue, but it is a social issue. Only one gender can not be abuser and other victim. Both sides of problem are to be acknowledged and addressed in our society. Some of the suggestions are given here to tackle the problem of domestic violence against men:

(a) Before enforcing any law, we should educated the people about its objects and usage. Due to illiteracy masses do not come to know about real objects of any law.

(b) Whenever any special laws are enacted, the procedure and definitions should be very clear and goals of law should be crystal clear.

(c) Gender biased law should be made crime based instead of any assumption that women are always victims and all men are abusers and born as criminal.[29]

(d) Words 'men/women' under Domestic Violence Act should be replaced by the word 'spouse'.

(e) No FIR or case should be registered without any *prima-facie* documentary evidence against the accused.

(f) For registering any case, the investigating officer should consider the evidence from both sides and then to decide whether the case should be registered or not.

(g) The special laws must have provision of punishment for abuse and misuse of laws and making fake cases and complaints without any evidence.

(h) Judiciary should play positive role in this concern. If a male approaches to court, who is a victim of domestic violence, the courts should consider the matter sympathetically.

(i) Government and non-government organizations should establish shelter homes or rescue homes for men, victims of domestic violence.

(j) Government should propagate the issue on T.V. and Radio that whoever is victim of domestic violence (not only women, also men) should approach to authorities.

(k) Proper training should be given to investigating agencies, so that when a man as victim of domestic violence approaches them, they should not make fun of victim and to properly handle the case.

Notes and Reference

1. UNICEF, Domestic Violence Against Women and Girls, Innocenti Research Centre, Florence, Italy, Digest No. 6, June 2000, p. 3-4.
2. US office on Violence Against Women (OVW)
3. *http://www/fullhyderabad.com/discussions/viewtopic.php?f=16&t=42254&start=0(visited on 11.5.2009)*
4. *Ibid.*
5. Richard Gellers: Who's Abusing Whom? Domestic Violence and Political Correctness, The Women's Quarterly, Fall 1999.
6. *US Department of Justice:* Special Report on Violence related injuries–issued in August 1997.
7. *Intimate Partner Violence:* Face Sheet, released by Centre for Disease Control and Prevention.
8. The U.S. National Crime Victimisation Survey Report, 2003.
9. Department of Justice, Report on National Violence Against Women Survey.
10. Survey Conducted by Government's Home Office in January 1999.
11. *Ibid.*
12. Vineeta Pandey, "*Spouse Abuse:* It is the Husbands Turn Now", DNA New, 20 September 2007, pp. 7-8.

13. *Crime in India:* National Crime Records Bureau, Ministry of Home Affairs, New Delhi, 2009.
14. *Ibid.*
15. Minanti Singha, "Men are being Harassed, says Women Panel", The Times of India, 19 September 2007, p. 1.
16. Zamir Uddin: View Point: Domestic Violence Act lacks Perspective, Central Chronicle News, 18 September 2007.
17. About Domestic Violence Against Men : available at www.dvmen.org (visited on 15.11.09)
18. *Ibid.*, note 16.
19. Act 43 of 2005.
20. Section 3 (c) of The Protection of Women from Domestic Violence Act, 2005.
21. *Ibid.*, Section 4.
22. *Ibid.*, Section 18.
23. *Ibid.*, Section 32 (2)
24. *Ibid.*, Section 17.
25. Source: *India TV*, December 20, 2006.
26. I*ndia TV* Journalist Sting Operation, July 6, 2007.
27. Decision of petition is still pending.
28. *http://mynation.net/study-report-indianhusbands.htm* (visited on 20.11.09)
29. Rajendra K. Gupta, "India Force", available at <*http://groups.yahoo.com/group/india-force*> (visited on 8.10.09).

Domestic Violence:
An Assessment of Global Scenario

Duraipandi Mavoothu*

"The first civil right of every citizen is the right to be free from domestic violence" –**Richard Nixon**

INTRODUCTION

Until recently, most governments and policy-makers viewed violence against women as a relatively minor social problem, particularly 'domestic violence' (DV) by a husband or other intimate partner[1]. But now such violence has been recognized as a serious human rights and public health problem. Because, violence is a daily reality, experienced in the home, workplace, and in public. Gender-specific forms of abuse comprise "aggression against and exploitation of women, because they are women. Many of these "sex-specific" violations are sexual or reproduction-related including rape; sexual murder; battery; 'honor killings;' dowry burnings; Female Genital Mutilation (FGM); prostitution; forced abortion, sterilization or pregnancy and sexual violence of any kind. Relatives or persons of trust or authority such as family members, community members, and/or state agents can perpetrate such violence[2]. Domestic violence (DV) and abuse knows no boundaries as far as race, religion, age, sex, geographic location, sexual orientation, or financial and social standing. Parents abuse children, children abuse elderly parents, husbands or lovers abuse women and women abuse men and other women. A study findings show that women in Bangladesh, Morocco and Uganda experience multiple and severe forms of violence by an intimate partner, yet a majority do not seek help[3]. Research shows that between 23% and 42% affected by domestic violence report that the abuse had an impact on their work performance[4]. Forty per cent of the women murdered in Israel were killed as a result of domestic violence[5].

* *Reader, School of Management Studies, Cochin University of Sc. & Tech., Kochi, Kerala, India.*

Domestic violence and rapes continue to rise in Malaysia despite several efforts made by the Government to curb the vices, said Malaysian Deputy Women, Family and Community Development Minister *Chew Mei Fun.* Statistics from the Malaysian police showed that the number of reported domestic violence cases went up by 505 cases from 3,264 in 2006 to 3,769 in 2008[6]. One estimate in UK suggests that almost one in every three women will experience some level of partner abuse in their lifetime[7]. The severe restrictions imposed on Afghan women by the Taliban were an extreme example of women being treated as private property. The severity of domestic violence as a human rights violation makes it as a micro level terrorism. It is nothing but a domestic terrorism or intimate terrorism. Afghanistan has quietly passed a law permitting Shia men to deny their wives food and sustenance if they refuse to obey their husbands' sexual demands, despite international outrage over an earlier version of the legislation. The new final draft of the legislation also grants guardianship of children exclusively to their fathers and grandfathers, and requires women to get permission from their husbands to work. "It also effectively allows a rapist to avoid prosecution by paying 'blood money' to a girl who was injured when he raped her". Human Rights activists say that it is contradicting Afghanistan's own Constitution[8]. Apart from as a human rights issue, domestic violence is a disabler of talent, disadvantaging a significant proportion of our population to achieve their potential[9]. The direct and indirect costs of it are high and drain economic resources from households and communities[10].

Awareness, perception and documentation of domestic violence differs from country to country, and from era to era. Estimates are that only about a third of cases of domestic violence are actually reported in the United States and the United Kingdom. According to the *US Centre for Disease Control,* domestic violence is a serious, preventable public health problem affecting more than 32 million Americans, or over 10% of the US population[11]. Modern attention to domestic violence began in the women's movement of the 1970s, particularly within feminism and women's rights, as concern about wives being beaten by their husbands gained attention. Only since the late 1970s, and particularly in the masculism and men's movements of the 1990s, has the problem of domestic violence against men gained any significant attention. Estimates show that 30 of every 1,000 females and 45 of every 1,000 males are victims of severe violence committed by their spouses[12]. A 1997 report says significantly more men than women do not disclose the identity of their attacker. A 2009 study showed that there was greater acceptance for abuse perpetrated by females than by males[13]. This shows that the intimate partner violence is there irrespective of the gender. May be the methods are different depends on the gender of the perpetrator.

DEFINITIONS OF DOMESTIC VIOLENCE

Domestic violence (DV), also known as domestic abuse, spousal abuse, child abuse or intimate partner violence (IPV) can be broadly defined as "a pattern of abusive behaviours by one or both partners in an intimate relationship such as marriage, dating, family, friends or cohabitation". Domestic violence has many forms including physical aggression (hitting, kicking, biting, shoving, restraining, throwing objects), or threats thereof; sexual abuse; emotional abuse; controlling or domineering; intimidation; stalking; passive/covert abuse (e.g., neglect); and economic deprivation. Domestic violence may or may not constitute a crime, depending on local statues, severity and duration of specific acts, and other variables[14].

According to India's *Protection of Women from Domestic Violence Act 2005*, domestic violence is defined as "any conduct of the respondent shall constitute domestic violence if he, - (a) habitually assaults or makes the life of the aggrieved person miserable by cruelty of conduct even if such conduct does not amount to physical ill-treatment; or (b) forces the aggrieved person to lead an immoral life; or (c) otherwise injures or harms the aggrieved person. In this act the term 'domestic violence' has been made wide enough to encompass every possibility as it covers all forms of physical, sexual, verbal, emotional and economic abuse that can harm, cause injury to, endanger the health, safety, life, limb or well-being, either mental or physical of the aggrieved person. This is a genuinely wide definition and covers every eventuality. The definition of an 'aggrieved' person' is equally wide and covers not just the wife but a woman who is the sexual partner of the male irrespective of whether she is his legal wife or not. The daughter, mother, sister, child (male or female), widowed relative, in fact, any woman residing in the household who is related in some way to the respondent, is also covered by the Act. The respondent under the definition given in the Act is "any male, adult person who is, or has been, in a domestic relationship with the aggrieved person" but so that his mother, sister and other relatives do not go scot free, the case can also be filed against relatives of the husband or male partner.

The US Office on Violence Against Women (OVW) defines domestic violence as "a pattern of abusive behavior in any relationship that is used by one partner to gain or maintain power and control over another intimate partner". The definition adds that domestic violence can happen to anyone regardless of race, age, sexual orientation, religion, or gender, and that it can take many forms, including physical abuse, sexual abuse, emotional, economic, and psychological abuse.

According to *Charles E. Corry*[15], "any act or threatened act of violence that is committed by any person against another person to whom the actor is currently or was formerly related, or with whom the actor is living or has lived in the same domicile, or with whom the actor is involved or has been involved in an intimate relationship". 'Domestic abuse' may also include any act or threatened act of violence against the minor children of either of the parties.

The US Justice Department defines domestic violence as "a pattern of abusive behavior used by one partner in any relationship to control another partner. It can be physical, sexual, emotional, or economic abuse – controlling someone's finances".

According to *Family Violence Prevention Fund and the Trauma Foundation*, San Francisco, California, "domestic violence is the actual or threatened physical, sexual, psychological or economic abuse of an individual by someone with whom they have or have had an intimate relationship"[16].

Linda Chamberlain defines Domestic Violence as "a pattern of assaultive and coercive behaviours including[17]:

- Inflicted physical injury
- Psychological abuse
- Sexual assault
- Progressive social isolation
- Stalking
- Deprivation
- Intimidation and threats

These definitions of domestic violence and abuse are rooted in the paradigm of domestic violence promoted by feminists. The innocent woman, powerless and trapped by economic or psychological dependency, is always victimized by the brutal, domineering man who uses force to impose control in order to maintain the patriarchy. Of course feminists completely ignore numerous studies showing that approximately 50% of the violence between couples is mutual combat and 25%-30% of the total is exclusively female against male assault. There is also mounting evidence that in the majority of cases (60%) where women are injured by domestic violence, the female initiated the violence that left her injured[18].

FORMS OF DOMESTIC VIOLENCE

All forms of domestic abuse have one purpose: to gain and maintain total control over the victim. Abusers use many tactics to exert power over their spouse or partner: dominance, humiliation, isolation, threats, intimidation, denial and blame[19]. The various forms are:

- Direct physical violence ranging from unwanted physical contact to rape and murder.
- Indirect physical violence may include destruction of objects, striking or throwing objects near the victim, or harm to pets.
- Mental or emotional abuse including verbal threats of physical violence to the victim, the self, or others including children, and verbal violence including threats, insults, put-downs, and attacks.
- Non-verbal threats may include gestures, facial expressions, and body postures.

- Psychological abuse may also involve economic and/or social control such as controlling the victim's money and other economic resources, preventing the victim from seeing friends and relatives, actively sabotaging the victim's social relationships, and isolating the victim from social contacts

TYPES OF DOMESTIC VIOLENCE

The three main types of intimate partner violence are[20]:

Situational couple violence: It is the most common form of intimate partner violence. It is the sort of violence that enters a relationship when a disagreement that turns into an angry argument escalates into violence. The violence can be mild or severe, and although often this is an isolated incident in a relationship, some couples have a recurring pattern of such violence that is extremely dangerous. Although this type of violence is almost as likely to be perpetrated by women as by men, men do more serious damage and their violence is more likely to introduce fear into a relationship and to get the authorities involved.

Intimate terrorism: It is the kind of intimate partner violence that involves a batterer who terrorizes and takes complete control of his partner through the use of violence in combination with other control tactics such as threats and intimidation, economic control, psychological abuse, isolation, and the assertion of male privilege. In heterosexual relationships, intimate terrorism almost always involves a man terrorizing a woman, although in rare cases their women partners terrorize men. Although intimate terrorism is much less frequent than is situational couple violence, it is estimated that more than two million women. are victims of this kind of abuse in the United States each year - and this is the intimate violence that is most likely to destroy lives.

Violent resistance: It is the violence involved when a victim of intimate terrorism fights back. This is the violence of women trying to physically resist domination by abusive men. It is often transitory because of men's usual ability to dominate a woman physically, and most women who resist violently soon turn to other means of coping with their abuse. All three types of violence can be dangerous, even life threatening, and some sort of intervention is called for in each type of intimate partner violence.

CAUSES FOR DOMESTIC VIOLENCE

"When families are experiencing stress, regardless of what creates that stress, sometimes people's behaviour becomes irrational and unpredictable"[21]. According to *Charles E. Corry*, most, if not all couples will have a fight over something at some point in their relationship. Finances tend to be high on that list but the origin of the fight may be something as trivial as where to go for dinner. Such battles are not the concern of society. But, in the rare cases when such fights escalate to the point where weapons are used and significant injuries are knowingly or deliberately inflicted, domestic violence then, and only then, becomes an issue for the criminal justice system. While there are many reasons, including patriarchy and male control and power, for potentially criminal levels of intimate partner violence, there are no simple and universal causes. While in some cases of domestic violence there is a clear and unique causative agent, e.g., a personality disorder, in most cases there are many related factors at work, e.g., substance abuse coupled with financial problems coupled with one or both of the partners being abused as children. Some clear associations with criminal domestic violence have emerged. The list below is factors that are associated with the domestic violence[22]:

- Single-parent mothers
- Abused as a child or raised in a violent household
- Perimenopause: the change of life
- Jealousy and vengeance
- Money and financial problems
- Personality disorders and mental illness
- Drugs, licit and illicit
- Health problems and injuries
- Disabilities and aging

CYCLE OF DOMESTIC VIOLENCE

Lenore Walker presented a model of cycle of violence which consists of *three* basic phases[23]:

Honeymoon Phase: Characterized by affection, apology, and apparent end of violence. During this stage the batterer feels overwhelming feelings of remorse and sadness. Some batterers walk away from the situation, while others shower their victims with love and affection.

Tension Building Phase: Characterized by poor communication, tension, fear of causing outbursts. During this stage the victims try to calm the batterer down, to avoid any major violent confrontations.

Acting-out Phase: Characterized by outbursts of violent, abusive incidents. During this stage the batterer attempts to dominate his/her partner(victim), with the use of domestic violence.

Although it is easy to see the outbursts of the Acting-out Phase as abuse, even the more pleasant behaviours of the Honeymoon Phase serve to perpetuate the abuse. Many domestic violence advocates believe that the cycle of violence theory is limited and does not reflect the realities of many men and women experiencing domestic violence.

OTHER CATEGORIES OF VICTIMS OF DOMESTIC VIOLENCE

The scope of the violence is not just limited to the female spouse, but also is extended to other categories of people. Such categories include rural and marginalized, immigrant women, teens, children, disabled, elderly, LGBTQ, and men.

Rural and Marginalised: Women in rural areas are a marginalised group. Although they hold a central position in the production of food at a world level, which reaches 80 per cent in African countries, 60 per cent in Asian countries and 30-40 per cent in South America and is increasing worldwide year after year, their role is not recognised in agriculture. Rather their rights are violated and no protection against the violence suffered by these citizens of the rural world. *The Standing Committee on Women Farmers of International Federation of Agricultural Producers (IFAP)* says that domestic violence is a reality in rural areas. The reasons are absence of authorities in charge of enforcing laws, the poor training of the existing authorities, limited access to health and law services, and precariousness in the provision of services[24].

IFAP, in 2005, has recommended the following to protect the rural women from domestic violence[25]:

1. To design innovative strategies in order to avoid this violence and ways to integrate this situation into health services in collaboration with the different countries' authorities.
2. To raise awareness within the population about the magnitude and extent of violence against women.
3. To create efficient local bodies in rural communities that take charge of women when their rights are violated.
4. To raise awareness about the conventions and other legal instruments that concerns women's rights.

Immigrant Women: Bob Free and Penny Fields (2003) say that perhaps the most vulnerable and marginalized of all people are the immigrant women who experience domestic violence. They are vulnerable not only because they are controlled and abused by their husbands, but also because they face possible loss of their children, may have no place to live, and can be deported from the host country if their husbands refuse to sponsor them for legal status. Unfortunately, abused immigrant women have great difficulty accessing legal help. U.S. men sometimes marry young women, use them for sex, and then try to have them deported just before the women can receive their green cards, claiming the women came into the marriage fraudulently. There are men who are abusive but the women don't report it for fear of being deported for not being a good wife. Surveys found that nearly 60 per cent of the married women had experienced physical and/or sexual abuse from their partners. Among the battered immigrant women in the survey, nearly one-third cited fear of immigration consequences as a significant barrier to seeking social and legal services. An abuser may also deny his immigrant wife the opportunity to learn English or pursue job training and other education that would allow her to achieve social and economic independence. Immigrant women frequently do not know their legal rights in the face of violence by their husbands, and the husbands may convince them that there is nowhere to turn for help. Fear of police, and fear of the law and lawyers, may prevent immigrant women from seeking help. Finally, a spouse may threaten children or other family members, informing the victim that if she seeks help from the police or courts, he will automatically gain custody of the children[26]. *Shahpara Sayeed,* a Muslim wife was burned to death when the taxicab exploded when she was with in it, allegedly ignited by her angry husband on August 24, 2000 in Chicago. The 33-year-old Chicago resident was trying to escape after reportedly being doused in gasoline by her husband, *Mohammed Haroon,* who then reportedly threw lit matches into the car. She had immigrated to the US only a year before from Pakistan. She had been married two years ago to *Haroon*[27].

On November 16, 2009, a 28 year old British Punjabi woman *Geeta Aulakh* was murdered in the west London suburb of Greenford within months of her leaving her Indian-born husband because of family tensions has fuelled concerns over the rising curve of domestic violence among Britain's south Asian community. She was a receptionist at the local Sunrise Radio and mother of two small children. *Geeta* was on her way to collect her two sons, aged eight and nine, from a child-minder's home when she was attacked. This incident confirms the worst fears about the extent of domestic violence in south Asian community in Britain as well as among native white families. *Geeta* was brutally attacked in what police believe was a "planned assault" by more than one person. It is suspected that she may have known the alleged assailants. Police have confirmed that on two occasions *Geeta* called the emergency helpline 999 but when officers arrived she did not lodge a formal complaint. Campaigners claim that her behaviour was consistent with the reluctance among Asian women to go to the police. "One, they don't trust the police; and two there is a cultural thing that Asian women don't go public with their private difficulties. According to *Geeta's* colleagues, her separated husband had been pestering her to return, and she felt "frightened" and "harassed"[28].

When people are living in a country illegally, forging documents and faking identities, they are less likely to seek help for their problems from the right venues because they are clearly living in fear. That means that couples that are having problems are not willing to contact social services for fear of being found out. The same principle applies to seeking medical help. Even worse, this culture of illegality doesn't just stop with forging a few proofs of identification. It becomes a way of life that extends to the business, the social and the family.

Teens: Abuse in dating relationships is common among teens. In the United States, 33% of teens reporting some kind of abuse and 12% reporting physical abuse[29]. Teen dating abuse is like domestic violence in adults in that it also is a pattern of abusive behavior used to control another person. Teen dating abuse can include emotional or mental abuse, sexual abuse, and physical abuse. For teens, relationship abuse often takes the form of extreme possessiveness and jealousy. Abusers try to manipulate their dating partners by making all the decisions, putting them down in front of friends, threatening to kill themselves, stalking them, or forcing them to have sex.

Children: Every year, as many as 275 million children worldwide become caught in the crossfire of domestic violence and suffer the full consequences of a turbulent home life. Violence against children involves physical and psychological abuse and injury, neglect or negligent treatment, exploitation and sexual abuse. The perpetrators may include parents and other close family members. Children who survive abuse often suffer long-term physical and psychological damage that impairs their ability to learn and socialize, and makes it difficult for them to perform well in school and develop close and positive friendships. Children who grow up in a violent home are more likely to suffer abuse compared to children who have a peaceful home life. Studies from some of the largest countries in the developing world, including China, Colombia, Egypt, India, Mexico, the Philippines and South Africa, indicate a strong correlation between violence against women and violence against children. The behavioural and psychological consequences of growing up in a violent home can be just as devastating for children who are not directly abused themselves. Children who are exposed to violence often suffer symptoms of post-traumatic stress disorder, such as bed-wetting or nightmares, and are at greater risk than their peers of suffering from allergies, asthma, gastrointestinal problems, depression and anxiety. Primary school-age children who are exposed to domestic violence may have more trouble with schoolwork and show poor concentration and focus. They are also more likely to attempt suicide and abuse drugs and alcohol. According to a multi-country study conducted by the *World Health Organization* – with girls far more likely to be abused than boys. Sexual and gender-based violence is prevalent in schools and colleges, with much of the violence directed towards girls. Working in someone's home can also entail the risk of violence. Child domestic workers – often girls under 16 – have indicated severe abuse at the hands of their employers, including physical punishment, sexual harassment and humiliation. Unlike other forms of domestic violence, women perpetrate much of the humiliation and physical punishment, although girls in particular are also vulnerable to sexual violence from men living in the household. The Report of the *Independent Expert for the United Nations* Study on Violence against Children represents a crucial step towards unmasking the issue of violence against children, including abuses perpetrated in the household. Its recommendations are comprehensive, with overarching precepts complemented by specific measures to combat violence against children in the home and family, in schools and other educational settings, in care and justice systems, in the workplace and community. These measures also include advising governments to establish an ombudsperson or commission for children's rights in accordance with the 'Paris Principles'. The report advocates for the establishment of a Special Representative to the

Secretary-General on Violence against Children to advocate at the international level, in conjunction with *UNICEF*, the *World Health Organization* and the Office of the *UN High Commissioner for Human Rights*, and the creation of a UN inter-agency group on violence against children, with representation from NGOs and children themselves[30].

The guiding principles of the Report of the *Independent Expert for the United Nations* Study on Violence against Children include[31]:

- No violence against children is justifiable. Children should never receive less protection than adults.
- All violence against children is preventable. States must invest in evidence-based policies and programmes to address factors that give rise to violence against children.
- States have the primary responsibility to uphold children's rights to protection and access to services, and to support families' capacity to provide children with care in a safe environment.
- States have the obligation to ensure accountability in every case of violence.
- The vulnerability of children to violence is linked to their age and evolving capacity. Some children, because of gender, race, ethnic origin, disability or social status, are particularly vulnerable.
- Children have the right to express their views, and to have these views taken into account in the implementation of polices and programmes.

UN said (on November 20, 2009) that the *Convention on the Rights of the Child* has become the most widely accepted human rights treaty in history, but 20 years after its adoption, much more remains to be done to turn its promises into reality for millions worldwide. The Convention articulated a set of universal children's rights, such as the right to an identity, a name and a nationality, the right to an education, and rights to the highest possible standards of health and protection from abuse and exploitation[32]. *UNICEF* Executive Director *Ann M. Veneman* says that the problem of violence against children is alarming with between 500 million and 1.5 billion youngsters estimated to suffer such abuse annually[33]. *Navi Pillay, UN High Commissioner for Human Rights* says "Children are no longer regarded as the property of parents or the passive recipients of charity or goodwill, but as rights-holders". The World Health Organization (WHO) estimated in 2002 that 150 million girls and 73 million boys under 18 experienced forced sexual intercourse or other forms of sexual violence. Also, the latest data available shows that some 1.2 million children are trafficked worldwide every year. *Pillay* says that the current global financial crisis is also taking a toll on children, undermining their survival, access to housing, health and education. When crises strike, social spending in programmes protecting children is to be counted among the first casualties of budget adjustments[34].

Disabled: Violence against women with disabilities can take many forms, which can occur at the same time. Some of them are[35]:

- *Denial of Care:* Denial of food, lack of or inappropriate personal or medical care;
- *Physical Abuse:* Assault, rough or inappropriate handling, inappropriate personal or medical care, overuse of restraint, inappropriate behaviour modification, overmedication, confinement;
- *Psychological Abuse:* Verbal abuse, intimidation, social isolation, emotional deprivation, denial of the right to make personal decisions, threat of having her children taken away;
- *Sexual Abuse:* Denial of a woman's sexuality, denial of sexual information/education (e.g. about birth control and childbirth), verbal harassment, unwanted sexual touching, assault, forced abortion or sterilization; and
- *Financial Exploitation:* Denial of access to and control over her own funds, misuse of financial resources.

It should be noted that the abuse could result in disability. Physical abuse may cause permanent physical damage. There are evidences that violence by husbands as causing loss of vision, and loss of mobility. Perhaps the single largest factor that affects the incidence of domestic violence against disabled women is the extent of these women's "families". Women who live in institutional settings, and women who are multiple or profoundly disabled, are most vulnerable to abuse because they are more dependent upon even larger numbers of people, and less able to get away. *Dick Sobsey* (1998) says that it is estimated that women with disabilities are 1.5 to 10 times as likely to be abused as non-disabled women, depending on whether they live in the community or in institutions[36].

Sobsey (1998) adds that while a disability can make it more difficult for a woman to escape or report abuse, social attitudes towards disabled persons are probably a bigger factor in her increased vulnerability to violence. The way in which society views disabled persons handicaps these women in many ways[37]:

- They are viewed and treated as children, as lacking intelligence;
- Women with disabilities are considered to be non-sexual and are often not given sex education, which can result in an inability to distinguish between abusive behaviour and normal or necessary forms of touching;
- They may be considered incompetent witnesses by police and the courts, particularly if they have difficulty or require assistance in communicating; and
- When they do report abuse, they may not be believed.

Some of the suggestions to contain Domestic Violence Against Disabled Women are:

- Abusive behaviour against disabled women needs to be acknowledged as a social and criminal problems, rather than being considered just a private matter;
- Community living alternatives may be made available for disabled women; and
- Training in self-defense, assertiveness training, and sex education should be imparted to them;

Elderly: Domestic violence towards parents is often kept quiet. Domestic violence grown old is when domestic violence started earlier in life and persists into old age. "Late onset domestic violence" begins in old age. Some older people enter into abusive relationships late in life. There may have been a strained relationship or emotional abuse earlier that got worse as the partners aged. When abuse begins or is exacerbated in old age, it is likely to be linked to:

- Retirement
- Disability
- Changing roles of family members
- Sexual changes

According to a study by *HelpAge India*, an organisation working for the welfare of senior citizens, Delhi has left cities like Mumbai and Bangalore far behind when it comes to crime against older people. In Delhi, home to nearly a million senior citizens, crime against elderly people is four times more than in Mumbai and double than that of Bangalore, the NGO claimed quoting data from the police of the three cities. The organisation said of the total cases of crime against elderly registered in Delhi last year, the highest form of crime was hurting a senior (42.2 per cent) followed by murder and robbery which accounted to 35.5 and 13.3 per cent respectively. The woes of seniors seem to be basically sourced from their own children and relatives with as much as 52 per cent of them facing harassment for property. Nearly 50 per cent of perpetrators of such crimes are children and children-in-law, followed by neighbours and others (27 per cent), the survey said. The maximum number of property-related torture cases has been recorded in South Delhi, known for its posh colonies and tony residential areas, while 20.8 per cent of such cases have been seen in central Delhi. The survey found that while one out of eight elderly said "no one cares they exist", about 13 per cent of them feel "trapped" in their own homes. Abuse of senior citizens often starts at one's own home. But fear of family shame, continuous harassment and dependency on the abuser prevents the issue from going out of the four walls. The abuse also comes in various forms – physical, emotional, psychological and financial[38].

LGBTQ: Violence against lesbian, gay, bisexual, transgender, and queer (LGBTQ) people are actions which may occur either at the hands of individuals or groups, or as part of governmental enforcement of laws targeting people who are perceived to violate heteronormative rules and who contravene perceived protocols of gender and sexual roles. People who are perceived to be LGBTQ may also be targeted. Hate crimes against LGBTQ people often occur because the perpetrators are homophobic[39]. The Bishop of Motherwell in Scotland, *Joseph Devine* has accused the gay community of leading a "conspiracy" against Christianity by allying itself with Holocaust survivors[40]. In May 1999, the *Admiral Duncan*, a gay pub in Soho was bombed by a 22 year old former British National Party member *David Copeland*, killing three people and wounding at least 70[41]. Violent hate crimes against LGBTQ people are serious because they tend to be especially brutal, "an intense rage is present in nearly all homicide cases involving gay male victims". It is rare for a victim to just be shot, he is more likelely to be stabbed multiple times, mutilated, and strangled. "They frequently involved torture, cutting, mutilation... showing the absolute intent to rub out the human being because of his sexual preference"[42]. *Copeland's* motivation was to wage a war against ethnic minorities and gay people in Britain. *Admiral Duncan* bombing was a vicious attack intended to kill gay people. He attacked areas he believed to be heavily populated by gay or ethnic minority communities. However, in all three bombings, he injured white and heterosexual people. Over the last decade the LGB community has continued to be the target of homophobia and hatred[43]. *Johann Hari* (2009), an award-winning British journalist says that teenagers who are in - or just out of - the education system have carried out almost all the new homophobic attacks. It is not a coincidence that the schools are the one place where homophobic violence is still absolutely mainstream. Homophobia is "endemic" in school playgrounds and classrooms. A study by *Stonewall* found 41 per cent of gay children are beaten up, and 17 per cent have been told they're going to be killed (it's 10 per cent higher still in faith schools). The young people who attack simply take that culture out of the playground and onto the streets[44]. "This generation of infants needs to be educated. We hear youngsters as young as four and five saying 'Go away, you're gay.' It might be a word to them, but their parents need to pull them up and tell them that it's wrong. They need better education to let them know that gay people are no different." The *Stonewall* study found that in schools with a consistent policy of punishing homophobic language, gay children were 60 per cent less likely to be attacked[45].

Gay actor *Sir Ian Murray McKellen*, an English actor of stage and screen, was honoured for his work on behalf of homosexuals, when a century ago *Oscar Wilde* was locked up and put in jail[46]". *McKellen* has received a Tony Award and two Academy Award nominations. In 1988, he came out as gay and became a founding member of *Stonewall*, one of the United Kingdom's most influential LGBT rights groups, of which he remains a prominent spokesman[47]. *Oscar Wills Wilde* (16 October 1854 - 30 November 1900) was an Irish playwright, poet and author of numerous short stories and one novel. He was one of the greatest "celebrities" of his day. As the result of a widely covered series of trials, Wilde suffered a dramatic downfall and was imprisoned for two years' hard labour after being convicted of homosexual relationships, described as "gross indecency" with other men. After *Wilde* was released from prison he set sail for Dieppe by the night ferry, never to return to Ireland or Britain[48].

The Manchester based *The Lesbian & Gay Foundation* is working towards a world where the LGBTQ are free to live their lives without fear, without prejudice and without discrimination. A world where it is accepted and celebrated that they have the potential to change and improve their own lives and those of the people around them. A world where lesbian, gay and bisexual people are positively encouraged to be parents, teachers, police officers, clergy, elected officials, journalists, sportsmen and women- in fact, anyone they want to be[49]. On 27 November 2002, The crown prosecution service announced that perpetrators of anti-gay offences will be treated with "zero tolerance". The initiative, which includes crimes against transsexuals, will cover incidents regarded by victims as homophobic or "transphobic" - based on the service's definition of a racist crime as one perceived as racist by victim as such[50]. "Homophobic crimes strike at LGBs' right to feel safe and secure, and to abuse or attack someone because of their sexual orientation and gender identity is a hate crime which cannot be tolerated. The *Crown Prosecution Service*, or *CPS*, is a non-ministerial department of the Government of the United Kingdom responsible for public prosecutions of people charged with criminal offences in England and Wales[51]. *Johann Hari* (2009), an award-winning British journalist, says "the fight to win legal equality for gay people is almost won in Britain"[52].

Men: Very little is known about the actual number of men who are in a domestic relationship in which they are abused or treated violently by women. In 100 domestic violence situations approximately 40 cases involve violence by women against men. In US roughly 300,000 to 400,000 men are treated violently by their wife or girl friend per year[53]. Sometimes a woman gives false case of domestic violence to get divorce and also just to receive the sole parent pension, child support, parenting payment, rent assistance, a concession card and other benefits, and she finds she has much more money coming into the house without husband than she ever did with one. It seems unlikely that she will get everything she wants in a simple divorce. The woman who alleges of domestic violence receives free advice about how to end her marriage, financial matters, emotional counseling, court support, free legal advice, the availability of emergency housing for women, and what Social Security and Centre-link benefits were available. The court protocols and judicial bias are always against the men. Men in such a situation become absolutely devastated and shattered. They in such a state of depression even lose their jobs. They find they have no children, no assets, a reduced motivation and capacity to earn and no income, and they see no future. They also see the grief in their children's grandparents, uncles, aunts and cousins, who have been cut off from the children they've grown to love.

Charles E. Corry says that in US, one where one quarrel with his wife or lover. The next day she calls work and says: "my husband or partner and I had a fight and I don't feel well". Perhaps she has a visible bruise where she bumped into something entirely independent of his disagreement. When she shows up for work, company guidelines, or an overzealous feminist co-worker, get in the act. Her company or the co-worker notifies the police. As hearsay is admissible, arrest and a restraining order are mandatory. Under current law the charges cannot be dropped no matter what she says. As a result, he is homeless, and the only way to clear his name is a jury trial months later. If he pleads guilty, or no contest, the restraining order becomes permanent and he is under a lifetime sentence. Whatever the circumstances, without question, he, as a male, will be presumed guilty until he can prove himself innocent. In addition, he will be punished for the crime while trying to prove him innocent. Thus, he is guilty until he can prove himself innocent and, even then, he will probably be judged guilty by many just on the basis of her accusation. So not only is he accused ex parte but also he is convicted in absentia. He may also be punished by the court and required to pay for 'treatment' before his trial if he pleads innocent.

CURRENT GLOBAL PROBLEMS AND DOMESTIC VIOLENCE

Today the world is struggling to fight against global issues like climate change, terrorism, economic recession, food security and degenerative diseases, which aggravate the domestic violences in several ways. History says that a new global problem comes up even before we are able to solve the existing one/s. Sometimes, one global problem leads to another. Generally, there is a lot of relationship between global problems and social problems, and it is there in the case of domestic violence also. The details of such relationships are given below:

Climate change: Climate change affects people all over the world, but in particular, it negatively impacts the lives of women, who are particularly vulnerable to crop failure or natural disasters. At the same time, empowered women can be agents for change[54]. The threats of climate change are not gender neutral, says *WomenWatch*, the *United Nations Inter-agency Network on Women and Gender Equality*.Climate change needs gender-sensitive responses[55]. A largely ignored negative consequence of global warming is the expected changes in violent crime. Research has shown that uncomfortably hot temperatures directly cause increases in aggressive and violent behavior, including violent crime. Normally, most disagreements end without physical violence. That may change, however, as temperatures increase. Social psychologists have shown in laboratory experiments that simply being in a hot room makes people feel angrier than being in a comfortable room. Aggressive thoughts also increase[56].

Laboratory research has shown that hot temperatures can, when coupled with provocation, increase a person's willingness to hurt another person. Other research supporting the link between heat and violence shows that regional differences in violent crime rates are related to regional differences in ambient temperature. Many studies, some going back to crime records in several European countries gathered in the last century, show that hotter regions of a country tend to have higher violent crime rates. Interestingly, non-violent crimes do not tend to show this same hot region increase in criminality. A study in the April 1996 issue of the *Journal of Personality and Social Psychology*, Vol. 70, No. 4, 740-756 on regional differences in violent crime rates in large U.S. cities ruled out many other potential causes of heat effect on violent crime, such as poverty, population size and regional cultures supportive of violence. The study found that U.S. cities with hotter climates have higher violent crime rates[57].

Research has also found that hotter days, months and seasons produce higher-than-normal crime rates. The December 1997 issue of the *Journal of Personality and Social Psychology,* Vol. 73, No. 6, 1213-1223 reported on two studies that examined the relation between hotness of year and violent crime rate in the United States from 1950 to 1995. One study found that summer produced more violent crime, murders and assaults, than the other seasons. If high temperature were a direct cause of the summer effect, then years with more hot days (days in which the maximum temperature is at least 90F) would have somewhat larger increases in murder and assault than years with fewer hot days. This prediction was confirmed by the data. These two studies are particularly relevant to global warming because the data allow us to estimate how much violent crime rates will increase as global warming continues. As global warming progresses we can expect violent crime rate steadily climbing[58].

Terrorism/War Conflict: As reported by *Boston Globe,* a 7-year study of youth violence conducted jointly by *Harvard and Brandeis universities* debunked the commonly-held notions that youth violence correlates more or less directly to poverty, race, and gender. Instead, researchers found the most direct connection to violence in kids ages 7 to 13 is how much violence they've seen and experienced at home. The amount of aggression children witness in their parents is a powerful predictor of how violent the children will become, according to author *Kurt Fischer,* professor of education and human development at Harvard. And even without prestigious university studies, it's pretty damned obvious: kids who grow up in violent households are much more likely to use violence as a way of solving conflicts or getting what they want[59].

Experts say that two-thirds of women are exposed to domestic violence in Tajikistan. In 2002-03, about 90 women committed suicide. In the period 2001-04, 344 women took their own lives and their partners murdered 433. Along with poverty, some observers link growing violence against women in Tajikistan with the aftermath of the civil war of the 1990s, that led to the death of at least 50,000 people while 1.2 million became refugees or were internally displaced. Women, as ever, suffered disproportionately during and after the conflict. Apart from a general deterioration in the position of women, which one should expect during a civil war, women were specifically targeted by the Islamists in the Tajik conflict factions on 'moral grounds. Islamic behaviour and dress code were brutally enforced, thus degrading and dehumanising women. Sergei Andreyev, a research fellow at the Institute of Ismaili Studies in London says that moreover, forced marriages and human trafficking - mainly of young girls - became more acceptable during the war". Another consequence of the civil war, albeit indirect, is the increasing participation of Tajik women in drug trafficking: they are used as "mules" since they are least likely to attract scrutiny by law-enforcement bodies. Anecdotal evidence suggests that cruelty against women has recently become worse, with mothers-in-law treating their daughters-in-law as servants with no human rights. The executive director of the Gulrukhsor Crisis Centre in Khujand says: "The more society becomes civilised, the more the methods of violence will become contrived. Domestic violence exists and one can say that accusations by husbands and mothers-in-law have become more caustic. That is why domestic violence drives women to suicide"[60].

Angola, where domestic violence is so common, it is tolerated as part of marriage. There are no official statistics on the level of domestic violence in the country, but a survey by the *Angolan Women's Organisation (OMA)*, says that nearly 4,000 incidents in 2008 - about ten attacks a day. Moreover, a preliminary study, referred to in the 2009 United States State Department Human Rights report on Angola, recorded that 62 per cent of women living in poor suburbs of the capital have experienced some form of household violence. Domestic violence is not illegal in Angola - and on the rare occasions it reaches court, it is prosecuted under rape, assault and battery laws. During the war, women became the main breadwinners and heads of households. When the men started returning home, they found family and community situations fundamentally altered and their role and place questioned, and this has bred frustration[61].

Global Poverty: Survey research seems to indicate that there is more intimate partner violence among poor people than among those who are better off. For many people, this conjures up an image of domestic violence that centers on the "working-class brute" terrorizing his partner[62]. Families who experience domestic violence are often also victims of poverty. Half of homeless women and children report being victims of domestic violence. Research shows that a variety of factors may contribute to the poverty of women and children who have experienced domestic violence, including lack of affordable housing and accessibility to legal assistance. Some of the most significant factors are barriers to employment[63]. Many women's stories indicate a pattern in their persistent poverty and battering relationships[64]. Punitive measures against the abuser in many cases merely deprive the family of a wage earner and force the victims and the children into poverty.

Global Recession: Economic downturns can be difficult times for family relationships. Women, especially those who are pregnant or work part-time, can feel particularly vulnerable during economic downturns. Stress in terms of lost jobs might create family tensions, violence and divorce. Worries about finances can create additional tension and in some cases, where couples have already decided to part, problems over selling the family home can deepen tensions. Women's social and economic circumstances make them particularly vulnerable to economic downturn[65]. *Richard Gelles* (2009) at the *University of Pennsylvania*, who studies domestic violence, says recession may not increase in domestic killings. But may increase in other kinds of abuse. He also says the economic situation will make it more difficult for some victims to leave abusive relationships[66]. Stress caused by financial pressures and job losses is likely to push more people into drink and drug abuse, which would result in a rise in domestic violence cases[67].

Mary R. Lauby and Sue Else (2008) say that economic stresses often lead to more frequent abuse, more violent abuse, and more dangerous abuse when domestic violence already exists. Domestic violence programmes report that victims experience an increase in abuse in part because out-of-work abusers have more opportunity to batter. Compounding the problem, domestic violence programmes face a trio of economic factors - cuts in government funding, increased demand for services, and decreased private donations as people lose their jobs or see a downturn in their personal finances. These budget constraints make it more difficult for local programmes to meet the needs of their communities. In 2007, the *National Network to End Domestic Violence* in US conducted its second annual 24-hour census of domestic violence shelters and programmes across the nation. The census report found that in one day, more than 53,000 women, men, and children across the country received services from domestic violence programmes. Over 25,000 of those individuals - more than half were children - found refuge in emergency domestic violence shelters or transitional housing. Yet tragically, on that same day, more than 7,700 victims who sought services from their local domestic violence programmes were not served because the programmes didn't have enough funding and resources. Programmes in Massachusetts reported 309 unmet requests for services due to a critical shortage of funds and staff[68].

Angela Hattery (2009) says that her research and the anecdotal comments by practitioners point to the role the economy and money play in domestic violence. At the micro level, couples fight about money and sometimes this fighting escalate to domestic violence. At the macro level, as economic indicators show rising unemployment, rising home foreclosures, and rising bankruptcy, two indicators point to a rise in domestic violence: (1) this year (2009) has housed more women and children in women's shelters than last year (2008), and (2) the rate of domestic violence and domestic violence homicide has been increasing. Shifting family dynamics due to recession is the perfect recipe for domestic violence. More men have been laid off than women during recession. Research suggests that men engage in intimate partner violence when their masculinity is threatened. One core component of masculinity is breadwinning. So, when men are laid off they may feel emasculated, which might lead them to use violence to re-assert their masculinity. This will be even more likely if they experience a "role reversal" and the wife is now the breadwinner, who expects him to take care of the home and kids while she's at work. The unemployment rate for Afro-American men is at least twice that for white men. Thus, this spike in domestic violence among them may be directly linked to the fact that the recession hit this community earlier than the white, middle-class community[69].

According to the *Texas Council on Family Violence*, 136 Texas women were killed by their intimate partners in 2008. That is a 30% increase from the year before[70]. "Whenever the economic situation turns sour it can seriously aggravate the relationships in any family"[71]. Emerging research from sociologists, journalists, trade journals, and law enforcement suggest that certain types of crime are rising and began rising in early 2009/late 2008 when the pains of the recession first began being felt. This has led some analysts to investigate a link between the two, theorizing that the anxiety, suffering, and loss of the financial meltdown has made criminals more likely to commit crimes[72]. *Johann Hari* (2009), an award-winning British journalist, says that in a recession, violence always rises, and violence against minorities raises more. Attacks on Muslims, Jews, and black people are also spiking across Britain[73].

Food Security: Females are more discriminated and show a very poor nutritional status relative to males[74]. Women's lack of empowerment is believed to be an important factor in the persistent prevalence of undernutrition[75]. The first project meeting, held in Jaipur, India, in March 2005, of *United Nations University – World Institute for Development Economics Research's[UNU-WIDER's]* project *'Hunger and Food Security'* says that the gender dimension of food security demands special attention. The effect of the status of women relative to men on various aspects of food-security can't be underestimated[76]. When resources allocated to women with and without the experiences of domestic violence are compared, no statistically significant difference between the mean calories consumed by the two groups can be found. However, there is robust evidence of women subject to domestic violence receiving significantly lower calories from the preferred food items such as, fish, meat, eggs, drinks and dairy products. Furthermore, this group of women is allocated significantly lower amounts of household food and non-food expenses compared to their counterparts who do not report domestic violence against them[77]. *Krista Jacobs* (2009) says that women in the developing world play crucial roles - as farmers and caregivers - in bridging food production and nutrition[78]. But these are the ones who are subjected to domestic violence and malnutrition. The emerging food crisis, partially due to climate change, may aggravate domestic violence, particularly in the developing countries.

Health Issues: Domestic violence is a major public health problem[79]. WHO says that domestic violence has association with women's physical, mental, sexual and reproductive health. Violence against women by an intimate partner is a major contributor to the ill health of women. Around the world, mental health problems, emotional distress, and suicidal behaviour are common among women who have suffered partner violence.

Healthcare issues in connection with domestic violence are[80]:

1. Risk of smoking or excessive smoking,
2. Excessive alcohol use,
3. Injuries and homicides,
4. Mental health problems,
5. Sexual-risk taking,
6. Lack of prenatal care,
7. Children of battered women are less likely to get immunizations, and
8. Poor nutritional problems.

Ever-partnered women who had ever experienced physical or sexual violence, or both, by an intimate partner reported significantly higher levels of emotional distress than non-abused women[81]. Domestic violence is a major public health problem in the United States. As many as 35% of women visiting hospital emergency departments for trauma care are there because of injuries caused by intimate partner violence. The practicing orthopaedic surgeon may come in contact with these women in the emergency department as well as in the office setting. The ability to identify victims of abuse requires a sensitive approach and a specific set of skills. Once the victim has been identified, appropriate referral to local agencies is critical to help ensure the victim's safety. The issues surrounding identification, documentation, inquiry about safety, and activation of community services need to be incorporated into the core curriculum of resident training programmes and the continuing education of the practising orthopedic surgeon[82]. Global financial crisis and war conflicts have worsened the health status of victims of domestic violence in resources-poor countries. *Dr.Margaret Chan*, Director-General of the *World Health Organization*, said (on January 19, 2009) that many low-income countries, more than 60% of domestically sourced health spending is private, largely in the form of direct out-of-pocket payment[83]. Economic downturn and war conflict increase the risk that the victims of domestic violence will neglect or will be neglected health care with prevention falling by the wayside. Less preventive care is particularly disturbing at a time when a rise in chronic diseases is global trends. A new documentary film "*Living in Emergency*" features the experiences of four doctors working in war-torn Congo and post-conflict Liberia. These stories are their intensely personal experiences, which are emblematic of the hard choices, dilemmas, and, sometimes, bitter realities that Doctors Without

Borders medical teams grapple with every day in more than 60 countries around the world". This 90-minute film has been screened on December 14, 2009 across US.

Health Care Response: Carole Warshaw and Anne L. Ganley developed a Resource Manual for Health Care Providers in 1996 and revised it in 1998. It includes[84]:

Information: To educate practitioners on the dynamics of domestic violence; screening, identification, assessment and intervention with victims of domestic violence; and interventions with batterers.

Practical Tools: Including a Model Hospital Intervention packet outlining effective protocols and sample forms for screening, domestic violence/abuse assessment, documentation, safety planning and discharge.

Ideas: To help develop and implement response strategies and programmes within a variety of health care practices and settings.

GLOBAL EFFORTS AGAINST DOMESTIC VIOLENCE

As governments and international agencies are taking up the domestic violence seriously, global efforts and integrated responses are intensified. Following are some of the global efforts against domestic violence:

1. *Coordinated Response:* The Domestic Violence (DV) movement is around three decades old and has accomplished much in increasing public awareness, in getting protective laws enacted and creating an extensive network of services around the country[85]. In the U.S the *Violence Against Women Act,* has successfully worked to create a national coordinated response to violence experienced by women, children and families across the U.S[86].
2. *Mass Mission:* Government of India's Minister of Women and Child Development *Krishna Tirath* said (on November 13, 2009), "about 28 lakh Anganwadi workers are being involved to make the women aware of their rights protecting them from domestic hostility and other women empowerment issues." Government of India is already working for National Mission for Women to provide a single window delivery of all women related schemes and redressal of their grievances[87].
3. *Religious Support:* Alarmed at the increasing instances of violence against women and children, the Catholic Church has launched an awareness campaign. ''The campaign is being organised by the Women's Commission of Mumbai, India, an arm of the Catholic church which operates through women's cells in parishes. According to community members, it was the United Nation's `Elimination of violence against women' campaign that prompted the church authorities to launch its own drive against domestic violence. The

campaign was conducted in all parishes of the archdiocese throughout November 2009. With this drive, the aim to step up the efforts and reach out to a larger audience"[88]. So, churches and other religious organizations must be roped in as strategic partners in combating domestic violence.

4. *Child Rights: The European Forum on the Rights of the Child* aims to bring together the relevant actors: Member States' representatives, Ombudspersons for children, representatives of the EU Institutions, the Council of Europe, UNICEF and NGOs. The Forum will continue to assist the European Commission in making progress in favour of children. In addition, this year's EU-NGO Human Rights Forum, the largest consultation platform for EU cooperation with civil society, was devoted to discussing children's rights. In the next years, the action of the European Commission in this area will focus on priority fields: violence against children, children in armed conflicts, poverty and children in particularly vulnerable situations (e.g. unaccompanied minors, Roma), the invisible children (including child labour and child trafficking). Efforts will also be strengthened to ensure that children themselves are given the opportunity to voice their opinions. In addition, a thorough evaluation of the impact of EU actions in the field of children's rights will be conducted in 2010[89].

5. *The U.N. Development Fund for Women (UNIFEM):* UNIFEM has launched a campaign in the Kenyan capital Nairobi to mobilise people around the world to take part in a drive to stop the pandemic of violence suffered by women. The global advocacy initiative Say NO - UNiTE to End Violence against Women, will stimulate, count and showcase actions on ending violence against women. The innovative platform will spotlight global efforts and demonstrate the groundswell of support and actions on the issue. The multi-year initiative will contribute through advocacy and outreach to the high-profile U.N. Secretary-General-led campaign UNiTE to End Violence against Women. The initial target of the plan is to reach 1,00,000 actions by March 2010 and 1 million in one year. Actions to be showcased and counted can range from reaching out to students at schools, to volunteering at local shelters, advocating for legislation or donating funds towards programmes that protect women and girls from violence. The luxury watch manufacturer OMEGA announced a challenge grant of $50,000 for the first 50,000 actions, a result of cooperation with UNIFEM Goodwill Ambassador Nicole Kidman. The money will go to organisations working on the ground[90].

6. *Awareness:* In US, the National Council for Research on Women is raising awareness about the status of women in the U.S. and globally by focusing on the Big Five issues of importance to women and girls,

namely: economic security, health, immigration, violence, and education. Although these issues are critical to the lives and well being of women and girls, they are particularly acute for those living in poverty, immigrants and women of colour[91]. UNIFEM also takes many initiatives that aim to raise global awareness on the issue and to make it a top priority for governments worldwide.

7. *Message to Police:* The first time in history a law enforcement agency has paid damages for their role in a domestic violence homicide of *Maria Teresa Macias*. In the $15 million federal civil rights case of Estate of Maria Teresa Macias vs. Sonoma County Sheriff Mark Ihde (Case No. C 96 3658 SI), the Sonoma County Sheriff's Department agreed to pay $1 million to end the lawsuit. With the force of the historic $1 million pay-out behind it, the case sends police the clear message that to continue their practice of treating domestic violence as an annoyance rather than a crime will cost them millions. *Teresa Macias* filed over 20 complaints with the police against her estranged husband for his violations of a restraining order, but police inaction allowed him to take both of their lives. *Tanya Brannan*, a journalist and activist, played the key role in the damage suit.
8. *Assistance for Immigrants: Northwest Immigrant Rights Project (NWIRP):* NWIRP, founded in 1984, is a nonprofit legal-services office that provides legal representation and community education to low-income refugees and immigrants in Washington State. Originally set up to file political-asylum petitions for Salvadorans and Guatemalans fleeing war in their home country, the organization has expanded over the years to serve immigrants from every continent except Antarctica.

Immigrant Families Advocacy Project (IFAP): IFAP was founded at the *University of Washington School of Law* in 1996 by Professor Anita Ramasastry. During the school year, IFAP recruits from 50 to 70 UW student volunteers to work in pairs under the supervision of pro bono attorneys handling VAWA cases. Formed in partnership with NWIRP's DV Unit, the organization was run without a budget for its first four years, wholly dependent on personal financial contributions from both Ramasastry and involved UW student volunteers[92].

Emerging Trends in Domestic Violence

New trends are emerging in domestic violence due to changes in laws, demography, awareness, women empowerment, etc. The new trends are discussed below:

- *Changing Scope of DV:* Today domestic violence is something that happens to many people who suppose, they are victims: although what happen do not make them feel like victims. It is not necessarily that the aggressor must be the partner or son. The aggressor can be even the wife or daughter. Pulling the hair, bruising the legs or hands, tearing off specs, lashing out, kicking, screaming, etc. are done even by daughters or wives. It is also a big problem in the family, but it is a hidden problem because it's not talked about. The United States Center for Disease Control has looked at the definition of domestic violence and concludes: "In recent years, the term 'domestic violence' has begun to include other forms of violence including abuse of elders, children, and siblings. The term 'domestic violence' also tends to overlook male victims and violence between same-sex partners. Therefore the more specific term 'intimate partner violence'(IPV) has become more popular. IPV is defined as "an actual or threatened physical or sexual violence, or psychological/emotional abuse by a spouse, ex-spouse, boyfriend/girlfriend, ex-boyfriend/ex-girlfriend, or date. Some of the common terms that are used to describe intimate partner violence are domestic abuse, spouse abuse, domestic violence, courtship violence, battering, marital rape, and date rape"[93].

- *Changing Laws:* A decade ago, some evidence of abuse was required. Someone had to show bruises, or bring in testimony to support the accusation. Under present laws (in US) a male need not do anything. All that is required is that a woman say, subjectively, that she is 'fearful' of her partner or a man she has known carnally, simply dated (with or without sexual congress), or even that she is related to a woman the man has known. Very likely she can then obtain restraining orders ex parte (without telling him) under current domestic abuse or stalking statutes[94].
- *Changing Methods of DV:* The more we become civilised, the more the methods of domestic violence will become contrived and sophisticated. The traditional methods of domestic violence are physical, sexual, and stalking. But the new trends are psychological/emotional and economic violence which includes extreme possessiveness, forced isolation, and destruction of belongings, taking away the car keys or locking the victim in the home, controls access to the all of the victim's resources, such as time, transportation, food, clothing, shelter, insurance, and money. For example, he may interfere with her ability to become self-sufficient, and insist that he controls all of the finances. When the victim leaves the violent relationship, the perpetrator may use economics as a way to maintain control or force her to return.
- *Changing Response to DV:* In the past, the response to domestic violence used to come mainly from feminist organizations only. But now the responses from other corners are also emerging. Politicians, bureaucrats, legal authorities, religious organizations and health care professionals also started responding to it. It is a healthy trend. In addition to this, the international bodies are also taking global efforts.

- *From Acceptance to Resistance:* Women's attitude has changed from 'acceptance to resistance' in relation to domestic violence[95]. Women have broken the silence and are coming out openly.
- *Intellectual Resources:* Compared to past now women are participating in careful research, networks and association to address and solve their own problems, especially about the domestic violence. Now they can do it independent of men.
- *Corporate Sponsorship against DV:* Corporates are joining the fight against the domestic violence. They give their supports and efforts to the NGOs and other woman organizations. For example, Verizon Wireless, an US based telecommunications company, provides 24 hours toll-free hotline support to individuals who are in imminent danger by linking them to domestic violence shelters in their calling area in Florida.

GROWING INTEGRATED RESPONSE TO DOMESTIC VIOLENCE

Christine Foreman (2002) says that for some time, there has been much dissatisfaction around the options available for dealing with incidents of domestic (family) violence and the issues involved in it. Several strategies have been employed to achieve increased awareness of domestic violence, its criminality and knowledge of related issues and support services, amongst service providers and members of the general public[96]. *Sandra J. Clark et.al.* (1996) Says that there is a growing awareness that the problem of violence against women is complex and requires comprehensive service responses involving agencies and services beyond the justice systems[97]. The needs of battered women and their batterers span several service systems, and may require interventions by one or more of the criminal and civil justice systems, social service, health, or mental health care agencies, and support systems for battered women and their families. Battered women sometimes seek relief through the criminal justice system, which historically has served as the main vehicle in a community's formal response to domestic violence. They may also access domestic violence shelters and services instead of, or in addition to, criminal justice measures. In many communities, the services may be inadequate to serve all battered women who request services from the shelter. The health care system often unwittingly provides another important source of services for battered women, although traditionally it has not played an active role in identifying or intervening in domestic violence. In recent years some health care providers have become increasingly aware of this issue and have developed policies to screen for domestic violence and to intervene in these cases. Health care systems represent important intervention points for expansion of community-wide systems of response to domestic violence, but attempts to use them this way will raise many important issues that do not surface when women themselves identify battering as the problem. Other service systems such as alcohol and drug treatment programmes, child protective services, and programmes for the homeless are also very likely to have clients who suffer from domestic violence, and may also have clients who are perpetrators. The past two decades have seen dramatic changes in the response to domestic violence in states and communities throughout the United States. A great deal of the change has occurred within the criminal and civil justice systems. In many communities the justice systems have experienced a number of important changes in their laws and agency practices related to domestic violence. As a result many justice systems now respond to domestic violence in a way that is more likely than in the past to hold perpetrators accountable and to protect and support battered women. At the same time, social services for battered women have become more widely available with substantial growth in domestic violence hotlines and shelter services, and batterer intervention programmes have been developed and made available in many communities. While problems of execution and service availability still remain even in the most progressive jurisdictions, shifts in public knowledge and attitudes have occurred that, at the local level, seem to support better responses to domestic violence in many communities. A number of coordinated efforts have grown up over the recent past, as some communities have moved beyond changes in individual agencies, usually those in the justice systems, to respond to domestic violence in a more comprehensive and coordinated way. Many of the early efforts focused on coordination among agencies within the criminal justice system, or between these agencies and domestic violence service providers. In recent years, however, a "second generation" of coordinated responses has developed as some communities have expanded their efforts to include a broader array of agencies and stakeholders, including health care providers, child welfare agencies, substance abuse services, clergy, and business. Some communities have gone a step further and worked to involve the community as a whole in responding to domestic violence through prevention and education efforts aimed at raising community awareness and reshaping attitudes about this issue. Many of these more expansive efforts are quite new. The *Domestic Abuse Intervention Project* (DAIP) in Duluth, Minnesota is a nationally- known model of coordinated community response to domestic violence. DAIP has received extensive publicity, is widely known, and conducts much training related to domestic violence for criminal justice and other agency personnel from all over the United States and abroad[98].

Since the early 1980's, activists in the battered women's movement have been working to make reforms in the criminal justice system to create a more responsive, consistent and coordinated effort to address domestic violence cases[99]. Reform efforts have focused on reducing cultural supports for battering and shifting the responsibility for holding batterers accountable for their use of violence from the victim to the community (*Pence and Shepard, 1988*)[100]. While initial efforts focused on reforming individual components of the justice system, concerns about fragmentation and the absence of a shared vision and public accountability, led to the development of coordinated community responses to domestic violence (Hart, 1995)[101]. In recent years more attention has been given to broadening the response to include other community agencies, such as health care facilities, child welfare agencies, substance abuse treatment agencies, and religious institutions (*Clark, Burt, Schulte and Maguire, 1996*)[102]. A comprehensive community response requires that other social problems that contribute to violence be addressed (e.g., poverty, adequate housing, affordable childcare, and child support enforcement)[103]. A coordinated community response involves police, prosecutors, probation officers, battered women's advocates, counselors and judges in developing and implementing polices and procedures that improve interagency coordination and lead to more uniform responses to domestic violence cases. Components of a coordinated community response include: pro-arrest or mandatory arrest policies; follow-up support and advocacy for victims; aggressive and prompt prosecution; active monitoring of offender compliance with probation conditions; court mandated participation in batterer rehabilitation programmes; and monitoring of the system-wide response to domestic violence cases. Removing barriers to obtaining orders of protection, improving their enforcement, has strengthened civil remedies and requiring participation in batterer rehabilitation programmes. Specific policies and practices vary depending upon state legislation, the structure of the court system, and the characteristics of local agencies[104]. States and local communities have adopted different mechanisms for coordinating interagency intervention to address domestic violence.

The three types of coordination, which may be used with each other, are (1) community intervention projects; (2) criminal justice system-based reform projects; and (3) coordinating council[105]:

Community Intervention Projects: Community Intervention Projects (CIP) is advocacy organizations that focus on reforming, improving, and coordinating institutional responses to domestic violence within a community. They are distinguished from coordinating councils and criminal justice-based reform projects in that they are nonprofit agencies that are external to the criminal justice system and rooted in the battered women's movement. The eight key components of community intervention projects[106]: (1) creating a philosophical approach that centralizes victim safety; (2) developing polices and protocols that enhance victim safety; (3) enhancing networking among service providers; (4) building monitoring and tracking systems that strengthen system accountability; (5) advocating for battered women within the criminal justice system and the broader community to insure a supportive infrastructure; (6) providing sanctions and rehabilitation opportunities for abusers; (7) undoing the harm violence to women does to children; and (8) evaluating the coordinated community response for victim safety and offender accountability[107].

Criminal Justice System-Based Reform Projects: Leadership to coordinate the response to domestic violence may also come from within the criminal justice system. Innovative programmes that focus on integrated case management are often located within prosecutors' offices, although probation or the judiciary may initiate them. Also reforms, such as pro-arrest policies, vigorous prosecution, and closely supervised probation that include batterer treatment. Restraining orders can widely be used and violations can be prosecuted[108].

Coordinating Councils: Coordinating councils (also known as domestic violence councils, task forces or committees) can be formed in many communities to provide a forum for interagency communication and collaboration[109]. *Carlson* (1997) says that the Council can sponsor successful conferences, established working committees, developed medical and probation protocols, publish a domestic violence death review report, and implement a programme to provide victims with emergency electronic systems to alert police in case of danger[110]. An Urban Institute study of community responses to domestic violence in six communities found that all of them had some type of coordinating council (*Clark, et al., 1996*)[111]. The councils in the communities studied varied in terms of their membership, structure and purpose. For example, the San Diego Domestic Violence Council has representatives from over 200 agencies that provide services to victims and offenders. Subcommittees focus on different aspects of the community response: law enforcement; shelter and support services; medical; legal action; child abuse/domestic violence collaboration; ethnic concerns; treatment and intervention; grants and data collection; and education and prevention. In other communities, coordinating committees are more narrowly focused on criminal justice issues. For example, Baltimore's Domestic Violence Coordinating Committee is made up of judges and senior staff from criminal justice agencies. There is also a separate work group for front-line workers (e.g., police officers, advocates) to discuss coordination issues and policy changes[112].

SUGGESTIONS

The following suggestions are emerging from the assessment of global scenario of domestic violence. They are:

- *Income Equilibrium:* The income equilibrium between spouses will bring behavioural equilibrium. This will bring a strategic interaction between a man and a woman in a relationship with domestic violence. Both will try to maximize their utility and happiness. Even in a non-cooperative setup, there can be an optimization of the problem and the level of violence chosen may be low.
- *Utility Outside of the Marriage: Amy Farmer and Jill Tiefenthaler* (1997) say that anything that raises the woman's utility outside of the marriage, such as the availability of services or a generous divorce

settlement, will increase the probability that she leaves and, therefore, lower the level of violence if she stays[113]. This supports the need for an integrated response to domestic violence.

- *New Laws and Funding:* Lack of proper infrastructure and the mindset of the police are coming in the way of protecting women from domestic violence in Kerala State of India, one of the fairly developed states in India. Governments seem more willing to pass laws than invest in infrastructure to make sure it is implemented. Large number of cases gets stuck at the level of appeals in the higher courts. There should be a time frame for appeals in high courts to be settled. *Claire Wright* (2009) at the Thomas Jefferson School of Law in San Diego, California, says legal protections do not always cover all kinds of abuse. She also says abusers may simply change their method of exercising control, to try to reduce their chances of getting caught[114]. Laws must include all kinds of domestic violences/abuses. *Mary R. Lauby and Sue Else* (2008) recommend that we must provide services for every victim in every community, but non-profit organizations and the government cannot do it without a robust investment of private philanthropy and volunteerism[115]. In fact it is here the corporates can come forward as part of their CSR to sponsor infrastructure and other facilities to facilitate the response to domestic violence. NCRW says that the right of women to be free from violence is integral to the Universal Declaration of Human Rights. Supporting new laws and funding of the International Violence Against Women are critical for boosting women's safety and well being worldwide[116].
- *Responsible Fatherhood:* The issues for responsible fatherhood programmes are similar to those for marriage education programmes. The goal should be to help fathers who are at risk of situational couple violence to learn how to communicate effectively with their partner about the inevitable conflicts of family life and to manage their own anger effectively when necessary. Education about respect and equality in relationships (which is included in many programmes) can serve as a preventive with respect to intimate terrorism[117]. Lack of responsible fatherhood is a serious problem not only in developing countries, but also in developed nations.
- *Climate Change and Psychology:* Now the climate change has become a reality. Its impact on social change started occurring. *David Uzzell* of the *University of Surrey*, England, says, "Psychologists need to examine the attitudes and behaviors in the wider context of beliefs about environmental and social change". *Paul Stern* from The *National Research Council* (US) says that we must develop an international agenda for psychology and climate change[118]. More researches should be done linking climate change and domestic violence.

- *Political Will:* The solution to domestic violence is not rocket science. It isn't even feminism. It's just common sense. That fight requires, not millions more in tax dollars, but the political will to have police do their jobs and enforce the laws already in place to protect women from domestic violence[119].
- *Respect the Sanctity of Home:* President of India Mrs. *Pratibha Patil* says that committing violence against women should not be tolerated as it goes against the very ethos of civilized society. "The violence that women truly face both within and outside their homes is an aspect which is particularly condemnable and not tolerable as it goes against the very ethos of a civilized society." "Domestic violence violates the sanctity of the home, which is the abode of a love and affection. The enactment of the Protection of Women from *Domestic Violence Act in 2005* was an important step towards promoting safety for women and, in a way, of the whole family". The Self-Help movement has been particularly successful in enabling women to create economically sustainable models of growth"[120]. So, women must be considered as strategic human resource for national competitiveness and sustainable growth. This will free them from patriarchic clutches.
- *Men as Part of the Solution: Gary Barker* (2009) of *International Center for Research on Women* (ICRW) says that international efforts to reduce violence against women must engage men and boys[121]. This approach works well in Israel. Put the people(men) who are part of the problem into the solution.
- *Awareness of Physicians:* It is important that physicians are aware of the extent and pervasiveness of public health problem out of domestic violence. It is important to identify potential victims of domestic violence when they are encountered in the hospital or office environment. A few, short, carefully asked questions could serve an important surveillance and diagnostic function. Once domestic violence is identified, a well thought out, sensitive, safe plan of action should be discussed with the victim. In this way, not only will the current event be well managed, but also the potential for mitigating further domestic violence events will be initiated. There should be a broad education on the subject of domestic violence as well as activating victim advocacy among physicians and others who come into contact with this problem in their patients[122]. Health care professionals in the emergency room are an important contact with the victims of domestic violence, and timely identification and intervention can save lives. Overall, upwards of 35% of all emergency room visits by women are the result of domestic violence, whether due to acute injury, problems during pregnancy, or stress-related complaints. Unfortunately, domestic abuse is infrequently disclosed

voluntarily by the patient, and often overlooked by the treating physician. Thus, the purpose of this review is to familiarize surgeons with the presentation and management of victims of this hidden epidemic[123]. Ongoing training on domestic violence for public health professionals[124].

- **Inquiry as intervention**[125]:
- *Primary prevention:* For women who are not experiencing abuse, inquiry affirms that domestic violence is an important health care issue and provides an opportunity to talk about healthy relationships and the warning signs of an abusive relationships.
- *Secondary prevention:* In the early stages of an abusive relationship, early identification and intervention can prevent serious injuries and chronic illness as the violence escalates and the entrapment increases.
- *Tertiary prevention:* In relationship with escalating violence, inquiry provides the opportunity for disclosure in a safe and confidential environment. Even if clients do not feel safe disclosing their abuse, giving supportive messages can end their isolation and let them know that they have options.
- *Health Sector Response: Dr. LEE Jong-Wook,* Former Director-General, *World Health Organization,* suggested that the health sector can play a vital role in preventing violence against women, helping to identify abuse early, providing victims with the necessary treatment, and referring women to appropriate care. Health services must be placed where women feel safe, are treated with respect, are not stigmatized, and where they can receive quality, informed support. A comprehensive health sector response to the problem is needed, in particular addressing the reluctance of abused women to seek help. The high rates documented by the Study of sexual abuse experienced by girls and women are of great concern, especially in light of the HIV epidemic. Greater public awareness of this problem is needed and a strong public health response that focuses on preventing such violence from occurring in the first place[126].

CONCLUSION

Bad stuff may happen in any family. But still acknowledge that things could have gone better, while admitting that no family is perfect. Violence in family is definitely not good, neither it is the end of everything. We have to patch up our relationship slowly. Life is always volatile, but it should not touch the rock bottom. We have to get linked again in a joyful way for an ever-progressive relationship. Though domestic violence is a trivial subject and it should not be taken lightly simply because it naturally occurs and a private affair. Any society that tolerates or indifferent to domestic violence will lose its national competitiveness. The world has reached so far only the half-way point in responding to domestic violence. A lot to be changed in our laws, institutions, and mindset. Total empowerment of women, integrated response, involvement of men and corporate sponsorship may be some of the most effective strategies to combat the domestic violence. Women alone are not the stakeholders of their rights. The family, children, community, nation, corporates, and nature too are the stakeholders of women's rights. *Tanya Brannan,* a journalist and woman activist in US, who founded the *Purple Berets,* a grassroots women's rights group dedicated to standing with women who are standing up to sexist violence and discrimination said, "if we're serious about changing the world, we have to change women's world". *Herbert Spenser* wrote: No one can be perfectly free till all are free; no one can be perfectly moral till all are moral; no one can be perfectly happy till all are happy." "A woman was made from the rib of the man, not from his head to top him, nor from his feet to be trampled upon but from his side to be equal to him, under his arm to be protected by him and near his heart to be loved by him"[127]. If women are happy then the world is happy. Happy woman! Happy world!

Notes and References

1. *Violence against Women: WHO Consultation, Geneva, 5–7 February 1996,* Geneva, World Health Organisation.

2. *Fact Sheet of The National Council of Research on Women,* (New York). Available at: *http://www.ncrw.org/ncrwbigfive/wp-content/uploads/2009/10/i-vawa.pdf* [Accessed on November 28, 2009]

3. Murray Wardrop (2008), 'Recession will Prompt Rise in Domestic Violence', *Telegraph,* December 20, 2008.

4. Deborah Satyanathan and Anna Pollack, 'Domestic Violence and Poverty'. Available at: *http://www.familyimpactseminars.org/s_mifis04c05.pdf* [Accessed on November 29, 2009].

5. Ruth Eglash (2009), 'As recession deepens, social workers brace for rise in domestic violence', Available *at: http://www.jpost.com/servlet/Satellite?cid=1236603391690 &pagename=JPArticle%2FShowFull [Accessed on November 28, 2009].*

6. *'Violence against Women Still Growing in Malaysia' by ANI on November 26, 2009.* Available at: *http://trak.in/news/violence-against-women-still-growing-in-malaysia/ 28170/* [Accessed on November 29, 2009]

7. *http://www.bbc.co.uk/radio4/womanshour/03/200'9_02_tue.shtml* [Accessed on November 28, 2009]

8. *The Hindu,* August 16, 2009.

9. [3]

10. *A Report on 'Intimate Partner Violence' by ICRW & UNFPA in 2009.* Available at: *http://www.icrw.org/docs/*2009/Intimate-Partner-Violence-High-Cost-to-Households-and-Communities.pdf [Accessed on November 03,2009]

11. *http://en.wikipedia.org/wiki/Domestic_violence* [Accessed on November 23, 2009]

12. Sara Markowitz (2000), 'The Price of Alcohol, Wife Abuse, and Husband Abuse', *Southern Economic Journal*. 67 (2), pp. 279-303.
13. Kirsten Robertson and Tamar Murachver (2009), 'Attitudes and Attributions Associated With Female and Male Partner Violence', *Journal of Applied Social Psychology*, 39(7), pp. 481-512
14. [11]
15. *http://www.dvmen.org/dv-21.htm#pgfld-1000404*
16. *http://feminism.eserver.org/domestic-violence.html* [Accessed on November 27, 2009]
17. Linda Chamberlain (2005), 'Making the Connection: Domestic Violence and Public Health'. Available at: *http://www.endabuse.org/section/programs/health_care/_making_connection* [Accessed on November 04, 2009]
18. [15].
19. [11]
20. 'A Sociologist's Perspective on Domestic Violence: A Conversation with Michael Johnson', an interview by Theodora Ooms, Centre for Law and Social Policy, 2006. Available at: *http://www.clasp.org/admin/site/publications_states/files/0314.pdf* [Accessed on November 29, 2009]
21. *http://www.nbcdfw.com/news/local-beat/Recession-Fuels-Domestic-Violence–65082602.html* [Accessed on November 28, 2009]
22. *http://www.dvmen.org/dv-29.htm#pgfld-1310050*
23. *http://en.wikipedia.org/wiki/Domestic_violence#cite_note-94* [Accessed on November 26, 2009]
24. *http://www.rural-womens-day.org/declaraEng05.html* [Accessed on November 25, 2009]
25. [24]
26. Bob Free and Penny Fields (2003), 'Representing the Most Vulnerable', Washington State Bar News, December. Available at: *http://www.wsba.org/media/publications/barnews/2003/dec-03-free-fields.htm* [Accessed on November 25, 2009]
27. *http://www.soundvision.com/Info/domesticviolence/shahpara1.asp* [Accessed on November 27, 2009]
28. Hasan Suroor (2009), 'Blighted By Domestic Violence', *The Hindu*, November 25, 2009, p.13
29. Halpern C.T, *et al.* (2001), 'Partner violence among adolescents in opposite-sex romantic relationships: Findings from the national longitudinal study of adolescent health', *American Journal of Public Health*, 91(10), pp.1679–1685.
30. *http://www.unicef.org/sowc07/docs/sowc07_panel_2_1.pdf* [Accessed on November 24, 2009]
31. [30]
32. UN News Centre dated November 20, 2009. Available at: *http://www.un.org/apps/news/story.asp? NewsID=33029&Cr=unicef&Cr1=* [Accessed on November 24, 2009]
33. UN News Centre dated November 19, 2009.Aavailable at: *http://www.un.org/apps/news/story.asp?NewsID=33012&Cr=unicef&Cr1=* [Accessed on November 24, 2009]
34. UN News Centre dated March 11, 2009. Available at: *http://www.un.org/apps/news/story.asp?NewsID=30151&Cr=Child&Cr1=Rights* [Accessed on November 24, 2009]

35. *http://www.phac-aspc.gc.ca/ncfv-cnivf/publications/femdisab-eng.php* [Accessed on November 25, 2009]

36. Dick Sobsey (1980), Sexual Offenses and Disabled Victims: Research and Practical Implications, *vis-a-vis,* 1988.

37. Dicky Sobsey (1988), *Sexual Abuse and Exploitation of People with Disabilities,* Developmental Disabilities Centre, University of Alberta, Edmonton, 1988.

38. *The Times of India,* June 16, 2009.

39. *http://en.wikipedia.org/wiki/Violence_against_LGBT_people#cite_note-0* [Accessed on November 26, 2009]

40. Joanna Sugden(2008), 'Bishop accuses gays of 'conspiracy' against the Catholic Church', *Times Online,* March 13. Available at: *http://www.timesonline.co.uk/tol/comment/faith/article3545414.ece* [Accessed on November 26, 2009]

41. BBC News (1999), 'Thousands remember Soho dead', May 02. Available at: *http://news.bbc.co.uk/1/hi/special_report/1999/05/99/the_nail_bomb_terror/333913.stm.* [Accessed on November 26, 2009]

42. Donald Altschiller(2005), *Hate Crimes: a reference handbook,* ABC-CLIO, pp. 26–28.

43. Joanne Dunning (2009), 'The Admiral Duncan Bombing-10 years on'. Available at: *http://www.lgf.org.uk/the-admiral-duncan-bombing-10-years-on/* [Accessed on November 26, 2009].

44. Johann Hari (2009), 'Violence Against Gay People Can - And Must - Be Stopped', available at *http://www.johannhari.com/2009/11/05/violence-against-gay-people-can-and-must-be-stopped* [Accessed on November 26, 2009]

45. [44]

46. [40]

47. *http://en.wikipedia.org/wiki/Ian_McKellen* [Accessed on November 26, 2009]

48. *http://en.wikipedia.org/wiki/Oscar_Wilde* [Accessed on November 26, 2009]

49. *http://www.lgf.org.uk/about-us* [Accessed on November 26, 2009]

50. Clare Dyer(2002), 'Crackdown on homophobic crime', *The Guardian,* November 28, available at *http://www.guardian.co.uk/uk/2002/nov/28/gayrights.ukcrime* [Accessed on November 26, 2009]

51. *http://en.wikipedia.org/wiki/Crown_Prosecution_Service* [Accessed on November 26, 2009]

52. [44]

53. *http://www.oregoncounseling.org/Handouts/DomesticViolenceMen.htm*

54. Mahnaz Dar (2009), 'Al Gore speaks about climate change and family planning'. Available at: *http://www.conversationsforabetterworld.com/2009/11/al-gore-speaks-about-climate-change-and-population-control/* [Accessed on November 28, 2009].

55. United Nations Radio(October 02, 2009), 'Gender perspectives of climate change'. Available at: *http://www.unmultimedia.org/radio/english/detail/82926.html* [Accessed on November 28, 2009]

56. Craig Anderson and Brad Bushman (1998), 'Will Global Warming Inflame our Tempers?' *APA Online,* Volume 29, Number 2, February 1998. Available in: *http://www.apa.org/monitor/feb98/global.html* [Accessed on November 28, 2009]

57. [56]
58. [56]
59. Tanya Brannan (2003), 'Fighting Domestic Terrorism'. Available at: *http://www.purpleberets.org/violence_fightingdv.html* [Accessed on November 29, 2009]
60. 'In-Depth: Our Bodies - Their Battle Ground: Gender-based Violence in Conflict Zones'. Available at: *http://www.irinnews.org/InDepthMain.aspx?InDepthId=20&ReportId=62834&Country=Yes* [Accessed on November 29, 2009]
61. Louise Redvers (2009), 'No Law to Stop Domestic Violence', *http://ipsnews.net/africa/nota.asp?idnews=46672* [Accessed on November 29, 2009]
62. [20]
63. [4]
64. Jean Calterone Williams (1998), 'Domestic violence and poverty: The narratives of homeless women', *Frontiers*, FindArticles.com. 29 Nov, 2009. *http://findarticles.com/p/articles/mi_qa3687/is_199801/ai_n8772075/*
65. Amelia Gentleman(2009), 'Growth in Violence Against Women Feared as Recession Hits', *The Guardian*, March 04, 2009
66. *Voice of America News* on February 27, 2009
67. [3]
68. Mary R. Lauby and Sue Else (2008), 'Recession Can be Deadly for Domestic Abuse Victims', *The Boston Globe*, December 25, 2008.
69. *http://www.wfu.edu/wowf/2009/20091026.hattery.html* [Accessed on November 28, 2009]
70. [21]
71. [5]
72. BillShrink Guy(2009), 'How The Recession is Impacting Crime'. Available at: *http://www.billshrink.com/blog/how-the-recession-is-impacting-crime* [Accessed on November 28, 2009]
73. [44]
74. Vasco Molini and Maarten Nubé (2007), 'Is the Nutritional Status of Males and Females Equally Affected by Economic Growth? Evidence from Vietnam in the 1990s', *WIDER Research Paper Series*, Volume: 2007/54.
75. Kavita Sethuraman (2008), 'The Role of Women's Empowerment and Domestic Violence in Child Growth and Undernutrition in a Tribal and Rural Community in South India', *WIDER Research Paper Series*, Volume: 2008/15
76. *http://www.wider.unu.edu/research/projects-by-theme/poverty-inequality/en_GB/gender-and-food-security/* [Accessed on November 03, 2009].
77. Mohammad Mokammel et. al (2007), 'Domestic Violence Against Women: Its Determinants and Implications for Gender Resource Allocation', *Wider Research Paper Series*, Volume: 2007/80
78. Krista Jacobs (2009), 'ICRW to Congress: Women Key to food security and nutrition'. *Available at: http://www.icrw.org/html/news/news.htm* [Accessed on November 03, 2009].
79. Sisley, A. *et. al.* (1999), 'Violence in America: A Public Health Crisis—Domestic Violence', *The Journal of Trauma*, June 1999; 46(6) .

80. [17]
81. WHO Report (2005) on Multi-country Study on Women's Health and Domestic Violence against Women.
82. Zillmer, D. A. (2000), 'Domestic Violence: The Role of the orthopedic surgeon in identification and treatment', *The Journal of the American Academy of Orthopedic Surgeons*, March-April 2000, 8(2), pp. 91-6.
83. Remarks at the high-level consultation at WHO on the financial crisis and global health, Geneva, Switzerland, on 19 January 2009. Available at: *http://www.who.int/dg/speeches/2009/financial_crisis_20090119/en/index.html* [Accessed on December 10, 2009]
84. *http://www.endabuse.org/section/programs/health_care/_resource_manual* [November 27, 2009]
85. [20]
86. [2]
87. 'Mass awareness is must against domestic violence: Krishna Tirath', by ANI on November 13, 2009. Available at: *http://trak.in/news/mass-awareness-is-must-against-domestic-violence-krishna-tirath/23269/* [Accessed on November 29, 2009]
88. *The Times of India*, November 09, 2009.
89. *http://ec.europa.eu/luxembourg/news/frontpage_news/412_2009_fr.htm* [Accessed on November 24, 2009]
90. *The Hindu*, November 09, 2009, p. 20, Kochi.
91. [2]
92. [26]
93. [15]
94. [15]
95. Christine Choo (2003), 'Suellen Murray, More Than Refuge: Changing Responses to Domestic Violence', *Journal of Australian Studies*, No. 79, 2003.
96. Christine Foreman (2002), 'Integrated Response to Domestic Violence by the Criminal Justice System and Support Agencies in DUBBO', Conference on *'Expanding Our Horizons: Understanding the Complexities of Violence Against Women'*, 18 – 22 February 2002, University of Sydney, Australia.
97. Sandra J. Clark *et. al.* (1996), 'Coordinated Community Responses to Domestic Violence in Six Communities: Beyond the Justice System' A Report by of the Urban Institute for the Office of the Assistant Secretary of Planning and Evaluation, October, 1996, Washington, DC. Available *at: http://aspe.hhs.gov/hsp/cyp/DOMVILNZ.HTM*
98. [97]
99. Melanie Shepard (1999), *'Evaluating Coordinated Community Responses to Domestic Violence'*. Harrisburg, PA: VAWnet, A project of the National Resource Center on Domestic Violence/Pennsylvania Coalition Against Domestic Violence. Retrieved on November 27, 2009. Available at: *http://new.vawnet.org/category/Main_Doc.php?docid=379*
100. Pence, E., and Shepard, M. (1988), 'Integrating Feminist Theory and Practice: The Challenge of the Battered Women's Movement'. In K. Yllo, & M. Bograd (Eds.), *Feminist Perspectives on Wife Abuse* (pp. 282-298). Newbury Park, CA: Sage.

101. Hart, B. J. (1995), 'Coordinated Community Approaches to Domestic Violence', Paper presented at the *Strategic Planning Workshop on Violence Against Women*, National Institute of Justice, Washington, D.C.

102. Clark, S. J., Burt, M. R., Schulte, M. M., & Maguire, K. (1996), *'Coordinated community responses to domestic violence in six communities: Beyond the justice system'*, Washington, DC: The Urban Institute.

103. [99]

104. [99]

105. [99]

106. [99]

107. Pence E. and Shepard, M. (1999), 'An introduction: Developing a Coordinated Community Response'. In M. Shepard and E. Pence (Eds.) *Coordinating Community Response to Domestic Violence: Lessons from Duluth and Beyond*, Thousand Oaks, CA: Sage.

108. [107]

109. [107]

110. Carlson, L. (1997), *'Eighteen month report: Domestic Violence Council (1996- 97)'*. Santa Clara, CA: County of Santa Clara, California.

111. [102]

112. [99]

113. Amy Farmer and Jill Tiefenthaler (1997), 'An economic analysis of domestic violence', *Review of Social Economy*, Vol. 55, 1997

114. [66]

115. [68]

116. [2]

117. [20]

118. *APA Press Release,* August 15, 2008. Available at: *http://www.apa.org/releases/globalwarmingC08.html* [Accessed on November 28, 2009]

119. [59]

120. 'Violence against women against ethos of a civilized society: Patil' by ANI on November 13, 2009. Available at: *http://trak.in/news/violence-against-women-against-ethos-of-a-civilized-society-patil/23268/* [Accessed on November 29, 2009]

121. Gary Barker (2009), *'ICRW to Congress: Men and Boys Essential to Reducing Violence against Women'. Available at: http://www.icrw.org/html/news/news.htm* [Accessed on November 03,2009]

122. [79]

123. Guth, A. A. and Pachter, L. (2000), 'Domestic violence and the trauma surgeon', *American Journal of Surgery*, February 2000, 179(2), pp.134-40.

124. [17]

125. [17]

126. [81]

127. *NCRW Fact Sheets and Briefs (2008).* Available at: *http://www.ncrw.org/ncrwbigfive/violence/violence-against-women-global* [Accessed on November 28, 2009].

Status of Women–A Critical Approach with Refrence to Human Rights

N. D. Gowda* & Maruthi T. R.**

INTRODUCTION

Human rights, the most fundamental of all rights are the rights of people have simply because they are people. These rights belong to each person; man, woman and child. They are the right to life and liberty including all the political, civil, social, economic and cultural rights necessary for people to live dignified lives. Without human rights, people cannot live as human beings. Human rights are those requirements that allow us to develop to the fullest extent and satisfy our basic human needs.

Despite creating a dignified position in this male dominated society; the struggle for each and every woman is far from over. Although it's evident that women have left nothing unaccomplished, the percentage of women achievers to men achievers is comparatively low. Women are subject to prejudice by the dominant patriarchy and are in turn left out from supremacy.

The term "Women's human rights" and the set of practices that accompanies its use are the continuously evolving product of an international movement to improve the status of women. In the 1980's and 1990's women's movements around the world formed networks and coalitions to give greater visibility both to the problems that women face every day and to the centrality of women's experiences in economic, social, political and environmental issues. In the evolution of global women's movement, the term "Women's human rights" has served as a locus for praxis, that is, for the development of political strategies shaped by the interaction between analytical insights and concrete political practices.[1] Further, the critical tools, the concerted activism, and the

* *Faculty of Law, S.J.M. Law College, Chitradurga, Karnataka.*

** *Senior Lecturer in Law, University of Mysore, Karnataka, Mysore.*

broad-based international networks that have grown up around movements for women's human rights have become a vehicle for women to develop the political skills necessary for the twenty first century.

The position of women since long has been pitiable in all aspects of life and her subjugation by males has been throughout a matter of history. She could not feel independent, and act so, barring a few exceptions. Even today, the struggle for establishing her independent identity is being pursued though with more vigor.

The concept of women's human rights owes its success and the proliferation of its use to the fact that it is simultaneously prosaic and revolutionary on the one hand, the idea of women's human rights makes common sense. It declares, quite simply, that as human beings women have human rights. Anyone would find her or himself hared-pressed to publicly make and defend the contrary argument that women are not human. So in many ways, the claim that women have human rights seems quite ordinary. On the other hand "Women's human rights are a revolutionary notion.[2] This radical reclamation of humanity and the corollary insistence that women's rights are human rights have profile transformative potential. The incorporation of women's perspectives and lives into human rights standards and practice forces recognition of the dismal failure of countries world wide to accord women the human dignity and respect that they deserve-simply as human beings.

A woman's human rights frame work equips women with a way to define, analyze, and articulate their experiences of violence, degradation and marginality, finally, and very importantly, the idea of women's human rights provides a common framework for developing a vast array of visions and concrete strategies for change.

AN OVERVIEW

The Universal Declaration of human rights adopted by the United Nations General Assembly in 1948 outlines what is considered in this century to be the fundamental consensus on the human rights of all people in relation to such matters as security of person, slavery, torture, protection of the law, freedom of movement and speech, religion, and assembly, and rights to social security, work, health, education, culture, and citizenship. It is clearly stipulates that these human rights apply to all equally "without distinction of any kind such as race, color, sex, language or other status" (Art-2).

Obviously, then, the human rights delineated by the universal declaration are to be understood as applying to women. However, Tradition, prejudice, social, economic and political interests have combined to exclude women from prevailing definitions of "General" human rights and to relegate women to secondary or "Special interest" status within human rights considerations. This marginalization of women in the world of human rights has been a reflection of gender inequity in the world at large and has also had a formidable impact on women's lives.[3] It has contributed to the perpetuation, and indeed the condoning of women's subordinate status. It has limited the scope of what was seen as governmental responsibility, and thus has made the process of seeking redress for human rights violations disproportionately difficult for women and in many cases outright impossible.

The division between the so called "Public has compounded the difficulties posed by women's peripheral status within international human rights mechanisms and organizations and "Private" Spheres prevalent in so many societies. The pervasive division of life into "Public" and "Private" spheres has its roots in the desire to limit the jurisdiction of the government. In many countries, this has meant that what individuals do in the "Public" Sphere is subject to regulation, while activities taking place in the "Private" Sphere are thought to be exempt from governmental Scrutiny. Since this "Public" Sphere is seen as the focus of interaction between state actors and citizens, abuses of that relationship have been the focus of international human rights advocacy of course, the status of citizen has often been exclusionary, formally or informally entailing gender, racial and socio-economic bias and privileges. Thus, for those citizens-primarily men-who predominate in public and governmental realms and who enjoy gender, racial and economic privilege the issues of primary concern have tended to be those abuses to which they are most vulnerable abuses of civil and political aspects of human rights such as the violation of the right to speech, arbitrary detention, torture during imprisonment, and summary execution.

While women have been able to invoice international human rights machinery when they have found themselves in such situations, some of their specifically gender experiences of such human rights abuse-for example, rape in detention have not been visible within the prevailing definitions of abuse. This is because women have traditionally been relegated to the "Private" Sphere of the home and family, the typical citizen has been portrayed as male, and thus the dominant notions of human rights abuse have implicitly had a man as their archetype.[4] A major effect of the gender nature of the public or private split is that human rights violations of women that occur between "Private" individuals have been made invisible and deemed to be beyond the purview of the state. It is particularly important to note that gender is a significant factor in the decisions of governments to intervene in the so called private sphere to prosecute human rights violations. However, governments overlook much of what happens to women at the hands of men and male family members, for example domestic violence or confinement, even when there are laws against such abuse. Thus, abuses done to women in the name of family, religion, and culture have been hidden by the sanctity of the so called private sphere, and perpetrators of such human rights violations have enjoyed immunity from accountability for their actions.

The historical emphasis on human rights abuses in the public sphere and the concomitant neglect of the human rights of women were exacerbated by the politics of the cold war. The United Nations human rights treaties and mechanisms developed after the horrors of World War II and consolidated during the cold war. The purpose of many human rights organizations that developed along with them was to monitor the treatment of citizens by their governments and to ensure respect of citizens' human rights as they worked for democratic governance.

As human rights belong to all of us, is incumbent on all of us to protect the human rights. Human rights are about caring for other people in the same way that we could wish them to care for us. Each individual needs to be treated as special and unique. Human rights are for every body, even those people you disagree with or whom you actually dislike.

THE CONCEPT OF WOMEN'S HUMAN RIGHTS

During the United Nations decade for women (1976-1985), women from many geographical, racial, religious, cultural, and class backgrounds took up organizing to improve the status of women. The United Nations sponsored women's conferences, which took place in Mexico City in 1975, Copenhagen in 1980, and Nairobi in 1985, were convened to evaluate the status of women and to formulate strategies for women's advancement. These conferences were critical venues at which women together, debated their differences and discovered their communities, and gradually began learning to bridge differences to create a global movement.

In the late eighties and early nineties, women in diverse countries took up the human rights framework and began developing the analytic and political tools that together constitute the ideas and practices of women's human rights.

Taking up the human rights framework has involved a double shift in thinking about human rights and taking about women's lives. Put quite simply, it has entailed examining the human rights frame work through a gender lens, and describing women's lives through a human rights frame work. In looking at the human rights frame work from women's perspectives, women have shown how current human rights definitions and practices fail to account for the ways in which already recognized human rights abuses often affect women differently because of their gender.[5] This approach acknowledges the importance of the existing concepts and activities, but also points out that there are dimensions within these received definitions that are gender-specific and that need to be addressed if the mechanisms, programs, and the human rights framework itself are to include and reflect the experiences of the female half of the world's population.

When people utilize the human rights framework to articulate the vast array of human rights abuses that women face, they bring clarifying analyses and powerful tools to bear on women's exports to draw attention to human rights that are specific to women that here to fore have been seen as women's rights but not recognized as "human" rights.

The Universal Declaration states; "No one shall be subject to torture or to cruel, inhuman or degrading treatment or punishment". This formulation provides a vocabulary for women to define and articulate experiences of violence such as rape, sexual terrorism and domestic violence as violations of the human right not to be subject to torture or to cruel, inhuman or degrading treatment or punishment. The recognition of such issues as human rights abuses raises the level of expectation about what can and should be done about them. This definition of violence against women in terms of human rights establishes unequivocally that states are responsible for such abuse.

APPLYING THE HUMAN RIGHTS FRAMEWORK TO WOMEN

The Universal Declaration of Human Rights defines human rights as universal, inalienable, and indivisible. In Unison these defining characteristics are tremendously important for women's human rights. The universality of human rights means that human rights apply to every single person by virtue of their humanity; this also means that human rights apply to everyone equally, for everyone is equal in simply being human.

In many ways, this universality theme may seem patently obvious, but its egalitarian premise has a radical edge. By invoking the universality of human rights, women have demanded that their very humanity be acknowledged. That acknowledgement and the concomitant recognition of women as bearers of human right mandates the incorporation of women and gender perspectives into all of the ideas and institutions that are already committed to the promotion and protection of human rights. The idea that human rights are universal also challenges the contention that the human rights of women can be limited by culturally specific definitions of what count as human rights and of women's role in society.

The idea of human rights as inalienable means that it is impossible for anyone to abdicate her human rights, even if she wanted to, since every person is accorded those rights by virtue of being human. It also means that no person or group of persons can deprive another individual of her or his human rights. Thus for example, debts incurred by migrant workers or by women caught up in sex trafficking can never justify indentured servitude, or the deprivation of food, of freedom of movement, or of compensation.

The idea of inalienable rights means that human rights cannot be sold, ransomed, or forfeited for any reason. The idea of inalienability has also been important in negotiations over the priority given to social, religious and cultural practices in relation to human rights. For decades, work to transform practices which are physically or psychologically damaging to women and that have often been "Protected" under the rubric of religions, tradition or culture has been particularly difficult, given both the integrity of culture guaranteed by the universal declaration and the history of northern domination in much of the world.

Thus it was important that both the Vienna Declaration and programs of action from the world conference on human rights in Vienna in 1993, and the United Nations Declaration Against violence Against Women passed by the general assembly the same year, affirmed that in cases of conflict between women's human rights & cultural or religious practices, the human rights of women must prevail.

The human rights are indivisible is important women, Since their Civil and Political rights historically have been compromised by their economic status, by social and cultural limitations placed on their activities, and by the ever present threat of violence that often constitutes an insurmountable obstacle to women's participation in public and political life. By calling upon the indivisibility of women's human rights, women have rejected a human rights hierarchy, which places either political or civil rights or Socio-Economic rights as primary. [6] Instead, women have charged that political stability cannot be realized unless women's social and economic rights are also addressed, that sustainable development in impossible without the simultaneous respect for and incorporation into the policy process of women's culture and social roles in the daily reproduction of life; and social equity cannot be generated without economic justice and women's participation in all levels of political decision-making.

THE MOVEMENT FOR WOMEN'S HUMAN RIGHTS

The term "Women's human rights" does not refer simply to the theoretical approaches that women have used to transform human rights concepts, Programs and agendas. The concept of Women's human rights has opened the way for women around the world to ask hard questions about the official inattention and general indifference to the wide spread discrimination and violence that women experience every day.

While women have raised questions for a long time about why their rights are seen as ancillary to human rights, a coordinated effort to change this attitude using a human rights framework gained particular momentum in the early part of the 1990s. As women's activities developed globally during and following the united nation's Decade for women, more and more women raised the question of why "Women's rights" and women's lives have been deemed secondary to the "human rights" and lives of men over the past decade a movement around women's human rights has emerged to challenge limited notions of human rights, and it has focused particularly on violence against women as a prime example of the bias against women in human rights practice and theory.

The United Nations world conference on Human Rights held in 1993 was the first such meeting since 1968, and it became a natural vehicle to highlight the new visions of human rights thinking and practice being developed by women. The idea of women's human rights was a framework for women to articulate and collaborate around broad and similar concerns about the status of women; it also provided women with a way to elaborate on the most pressing human rights issues specific to particular political, geographic, economic & cultural contexts. By the time the world conference convened, the idea that "Women's Rights are human rights" had become the rallying call of thousands of people all over the world and one of the most discussed "new" human rights debates. The Vienna declaration and program of action, which is the product of the conference and is meant to signal the agreement of the international community on the status of human rights, states unequivocally that;

A particularly significant development was the way in which the platform for action at the IV world conference on women in Beijing in 1995 became virtually an agenda about the human rights of women. This signaled the successful mainstreaming of women's rights as human rights.

The most important international treaty specifically addressing women's human rights is the convention on the elimination of all forms of discrimination against women (CEDAW) which was initiated during the UN Decode for women and has been ratified by over 130 countries. Further local women's groups have integrated the women's human rights framework into their legal literacy programs and legal strategies.

The laws and conventions passed by the international bodies and the nation state have mirrored the world communities growing concern without laying sex based discrimination. It is upon the women half to make sure that such rights as are theirs should be utilized by them. The effectiveness of such laws and their enforcement depends on women themselves.

WOMEN'S RIGHTS AS HUMAN RIGHTS

Expanding on the provisions already agreed upon in the ground breaking 1979 UN convention on the Elimination of discrimination against women (CEDAW) the platform asserts women's right" to have control over and decide freely and responsibly on matters related to their sexuality, including sexual and reproductive health, free of coercion, discrimination and violence".

Then elimination of discrimination due to "Sexual orientation" was dropped because there was not enough support for its inclusion.

RIGHT TO INHERIT

Many delegates, who felt that traditional legal structures often discrimination against women in land rights, supported the equal right of women and girls in inheritance. Delegates from some Islamic countries argued that their religious inheritance laws, which were based in the principle of equality, mandated a distribution of assets that gave a woman half the amount that her brother inherited. Rather than equality, they defended the principles of equality. A compromise between the two positions in the platform emphasizes the injustice and discrimination women and girly often face and recognizes their equal right to inheritance. It calls for "enacting, as appropriate, and enforcing legislation that guarantees equal right to succession and ensures equal right inherit, regardless of the sex of the child'.

PARENTAL RESPONSIBILITY

The platform recognizes the "rights and duties of parents and legal guardians" to provide guidance in the exercise of rights of young people, but it also upholds rights of young people to information, privacy, confidentiality and informed consent on matters related to sexuality and reproduction.

REVIEWING LAWS ON ILLEGAL ABORTION

The platform commits nations to "consider reviewing laws containing punitive measures against women who have undergone illegal abortion". However, borrowing the formulation adopted in Cairo, it notes that "in no case should abortion be permitted as method of family planning".

Role of the Family

The platform recognizes the family as the basic unit of society. It acknowledges the "Social significance of maternity, motherhood and the role of parents in the family and in the upbringing of children". It also asserts that maternity must not be a basis for discrimination or restrict the full participation of women in Society.

Culture and Religion

Religion, thought, conscience and belief, the platform asserts, call "Contribute to fulfilling women's and men's moral, ethical and spiritual needs and to realizing their potential in Society". However, it also acknowledges that any form of extremism may have a negative impact on women and can lead to violence and discrimination.

Rape is a war Crime

Rape in armed conflict, the platform asserts, constitutes a war crime and, under certain circumstances, as act of genocide. It condemns "Massive violations" of human rights, especially in the form of genocides "ethnic cleansing" as a strategy of war and, rape as its consequences are also condemned. Such practices must be immediately stopped and perpetrators of such crimes "Must be punished".

Women many only have rights guaranteed by law but are often exercise them fully. This is due to failure by governments to promote and protect those rights. Mechanisms at national and international levels are also lacking. Women's rights are not secured in countries that have not accepted the convention on the elimination of all forms of discrimination against women.

The Judicial Response: Some Landmark Judgment

The constitution of India provides many safeguards to women and their rights. The preamble of the constitution provides to all citizens equality of status and of opportunity as well as justice-social, economic and political. The constitution imposes a fundamental duty on every citizen through article 51 a (e) to renounce the practice derogatory to the dignity of women. The question however is; have the women been able to reap the benefits provided for them under the constitution of India. The answer unfortunately is not encouraging.

The State has enacted many women specific and women related legislation to protect women against social discrimination violence and atrocities. In spite of all these protective legislations, violence against women, in India continues to rise every year, which is a matter concern.

The Indian Judiciary, Particularly the Supreme Court has played a creative role in providing justice to women victims of violence and has given for reaching and innovative Judgments upholding the basic principle of equality of sexes and tried to maintain the dignity and honour of women. It has been projected in a number of landmark judgments.

In *Nilabati Behera V/s State of Orissa,*[7] a provision in the International convention on civil and political rights was referred to support the view that there is not reason why these international conventions and norms cannot be used for construing the fundamental rights expressly guaranteed in the constitution of India which embody the basic concept of gender equality in all spheres of human activity. Further in *Madhu Kishwar V/s State of Bihar,*[8] the Supreme Court considered the provision of the CEDAW and held the same to be integral scheme of the fundamental rights and the directive principles. Art 2(e) of CEDAW enjoins the state parties to breath life into the dry bones of the constitution, International conventions and the protection of Human Rights Act, to prevent gender based discrimination and to effectuate right to life including empowerment of economic, social and cultural rights.

The Supreme Court of India in the celebrated verdict of Rupen *Deol Bajaj V/s K.P.S Gill*[9] has clarified certain issues as to what constitutes modesty and how it is to be judged. It is also a leading light in dealing with the issue of outraging the modesty of woman in this country and set a precedent for ground breaking verdict in Vishakas case which came a year later. In *Vishaka V/s State of Rajasthan;*[10] the vibrant judiciary has exalted the dignity of working women by issuing directions for providing safe environment at the work place to ensure protection of female employees from sexual harassment. In the absence of Specific legislation on the Subject, the Supreme Court took upon itself the task of preparing a comprehensive set of "guidelines and norms" and stressed that such guidelines be treated as law within the meaning of Article 141 of the Constitution.

An entirely new and very revolutionary illustration of Judicial activism is to be found in *Bodhisatwa Gantam V/s Subhra Chakraborty*[11] decided by the Supreme Court, The Court held that " Rape was not merely and offence under the penal code". It was also a violation of a women's right to live with dignity and personal freedom. It is not only a crime against the person of a woman; it is a crime against entire society. It destroys the entire psychology of a woman and pushes her into deep emotional crises. It is a crime against basic human right and is also violative of the victim's most cherished of the fundamental rights, namely, the Right to life contained in Article 21.

This Survey of Judicial decisions shows that the Indian Supreme Court has not hesitated in applying the international human rights law relating to women in resolving problems of violence against women and has been playing an effective and meaningful role toward protecting human rights of women.

CONCLUSION

Women may only have rights guaranteed by law but are often unable to exercise them fully. This is due to failure by Governments to promote and protect those rights. Appropriate recourse mechanisms at national and international levels are also lacking. Women's rights are not secured in countries that have not accepted the Convention on the Elimination of All Forms of Discrimination against Women. All governments must ratify international human rights, including the Convention of the Elimination of All Forms of Discrimination against Women. Develop a comprehensive human right education Programme for raising awareness about women's rights and also create of strengthen national institutions for protecting women's human rights.

Notes

1. Charlotte Bunch and Samantha Frost–Global Women's issue and Knowledge (2000).
2. J. Kerr, Women's Right as Human Rights (1993).
3. J. Peters, Women's Rights, Human Rights.
4. Rebecca J.Cook, State Responsibility for Violation Women's Human Rights (1994).
5. Amnesty International, Its in Our hands Stop Violence–Against Women (London, Amnesty International Publication, 2004).
6. Dr. Sarlagupta, "Evolving New Feministic Jurisprudence–Violence Against Women; A Policy of Neglect or Neglect of Policy", (2005) Cri. L. J.
7. 1993 2 SCC, 746.
8. 1996 5 SCC, 155.
9. AIR 1996 SCC, 309
10. AIR 1997 SC, 3011
11. 1996 1 SCC, 490.

Women under Labour Laws

MARUTHI T. R.*

INTRODUCTION

The predominant and pervading patriarchal system created disadvantages for women in every sphere and at all the stages of life. In reality, there is no doubt, that women all over the world have made tremendous progress. The social status have been improved, still the problems pertaining to their health, employment, social equality, social discrimination, violence, atrocity remains the same. Women's rights to equality with men is accepted and promoted in international development organizations and in the development plans and policies of many developing countries. The tensions and contradictions which women experiences in their unconventional work have an unsettling impact, unsurprisingly on their gender identities. The employment of woman has continued to be a problem since the early days of industrialization. The global profile of workingwomen as equal partners in economic and social is still far away from the truth.

It is important to note that during the last decade there existed wide divergences in the situation of women in the world of work. Due to global economic crisis and the aggravation of employment problems in recent years women have been seriously affected in the world of work. The economic factor plays an important role in status fixation in all these societies of the world. The comparatively lower status of women is considered to be the result of their economic backwardness.

SAFETY AND WELFARE

(a) Section 27 focuses that "no women or child shall be employed in any part of a factory for preserving cotton in which a cotton operator is at work. Provided that if the feed end of a cotton opener is in a room separated

* *Senior Lecturer in Law, University of Mysore, Karnataka, Mysore.*

from the delivery and by partition extending to the roof or to such height as the Inspector may in any particular care specifying in writing. Women and children may be employed on the side of the partition where the feed and is situated.[1] According to section 14 Beedi and Cigar Workers Act 1966 says, "in every industrial premises wherein more than 30 female employees are ordinarily employed, there shall be provided and mutual suitable room or rooms for the use of children under the age of six years of such female employees. Such rooms shall:[2] Provide adequate accommodation;

(b) Be adequately lighted and ventilated;

(c) Be maintain in a clean and sanitary condition;

(d) Be under the charge of women trained in the case of children and infants.

The state government may make rules prescribing the location and the standards in respect of construction, accommodation, fixture and other equipment of rooms to be provided under this section".

Women or young person shall not be required or allowed to work in any industrial premises except between 6 am and 7 pm. During last three decades, in many countries, the quantitative increase in the number of women working outside the household in paid employment has brought about the qualitative transformation in their economic, political, legal and social status. This is one of the most remarkable functions of this century; the precise economic and social causes have not yet been closely analyzed. A large number of women and children are employed in cotton and textile industry. Keeping in view more risk involved in pressing cotton when the cotton opener is at work if done by tender hand section 27 prohibits women and children to be employed. In Gamadia V/s Emperor[3] the Bombay High Court has held that there is compliance of the proviso to section 27 if door is made in the partition between the two portions of the room, which can be open by a women or a child employed therein. In order to protect the workers from health hazard the law has additional statutory restrictions on employment of women workers. Basically the Factories Act 1948, the Mines Act 1952 and the Plantation Labour Act 1951 prohibit the employment of women except between 6 am and 7 pm. However, the women workers on fish curing and fish caning factories are exempted from these provisions in order to prevent damage and deterioration of raw material. The rapid technological and scientific progress that is imperceptibly changing the world of work is linked to the intentional, national and the house division of labour, which cuts across the neat classification between macro and micro level problems. While there has been some progress in a few countries, which have promoted employment generation for women, adopted new legislation on equality and introduced special measures to eliminate discrimination between men and women at work and work place, women encounter may obstacles, which are special and specific to their status as workers.

Reducing poverty is political challenge. It involves overcoming class based interests in inequality and is requires effective public institutions to deliver resources to and create opportunities for the poor, frequently in the face of local opposition. When the poor women are the target of these kinds of interventions, resistance can be even more interest than opposition to pro-poor measures.

In Mine Act, 1952 prohibits the employment of women on any part time, which is below ground. Moreover, the Factories Act prohibits the employment of women on certain dangerous occupations. The reason for providing additional restrictions for women on three folded.[4]

(a) Women work in factories, mines, plantations or other industrial establishment in addition to their household duty find the long hours of work very strenuous. However, to prescribe shorter hours by law to women workers are compared to male workers would undoubtedly lead to the subtraction of men for women.

(b) The sex disparity in many big cities, which is already menace to the industrial workers would be further accentuated by an increase in the proportion of men employment while it would be diminished if women were more generally employed.

(c) If the hours of work are limited there will be less danger of their exceeding the capacity of Indian women.

The growing disparity between the female labour force, nature and type of jobs available and accessible in the labour market and women aspirating further strengthens the need to alter or modify existing legal, economic and social structures, norms and values. The Factory Act provides that no person shall be employed in any factory to lift, carry or make any load so heavy as to likely to cause injury. State Government may make rules prescribing the maximum weights which may be lifted, carried or moved by adjust men, adult women, adolescent and children employed factories or in any class or description of factories in carrying of any specified process.

It is important to ensure that technological changes in industry are directed specifically to increases women's welfare not only in terms of their employment, but welfare as well. It law be said that rationalization of production in the textile industry affects women workers in labour intensive parts of the production process. Women tend to be increasingly relegated to such parts of production, which are subsequently automated. This occurs within the context of increasing Labour mobilization. While the trade union efforts have led to higher wages and better working conditions, unequal labour legislation for men and women has led to a less favorable position for women in the labour market in the consolidation phase of an industry.

The technology policy must be carefully monitored from the point of view of women's employment. It is by now will known that with the introduction of modern technology women tend to get displaced even though the new technology could have been mastered by women. Labour legislations in all applicable spheres must be vigorously implemented. It is also imperative to have a review of the penalty clauses for the violation of such laws, for as expressed by some factory inspectors themselves, it is quite often profitable for a particular labour law and pay a small penalty as the implementation of a particular labour law turns out to be more costly than its violation.

CONSTITUTIONAL PERSPECTIVE

The Constitution of India guarantees equality of opportunity and status of men and women. It directs that women shall not only have equal rights and privileges with men but also that the state shall make provisions both general and special for the welfare of women.[5]

The role of the women's organizations should not merely be that of charitable or welfare organizations but should be one of active mobilization of women. In this there exists a role for the media and pressure groups in changing the perceptions of women about their work and status. Therefore, improvement of the status of women can be ensured only through their full integration and participation on the task of national development. Economic and social legislations are enacted for the betterment of the neglected class. But enactment of law itself cannot help those who are neglected unless they understood it. If women have to fight for their legitimate place in the society they will have to educate themselves and be familiar with various labour legislations. In *M/s. Machinnon Macharnzie & Co. Ltd. Vs Audrey D Costa*[6] the Supreme Court was called upon to interpret the scope of the expression 'same or similar nature' under section 5 of the Act. The Court laid down the following tests to determine whether the work is 'same work or work of similar nature:

"In deciding whether the work is the same or broadly similar, the Authority should take a broad view, next in ascertaining whether any differences are of practical importance, the Authority should take an equally broad approach for the very concept of similar work implies differences in details, but these would be defeat a claim for equality on trivial grounds. It should look all the duties actually performed not those theoretically possible. In making comparison the Authority should look at the duties generally performed by men and women. Where, however, both men and women work at inconvenient times there is no requirement that all those who work e.g., at night shall be paid the same basic rates as al those who work normal day shifts. Thus, a woman who works days cannot claim equality with a man on higher basic rate for working nights on that rate to, and the applicant herself would be entitled to that rate if she change shifts.

The Court added:

"We do not suggest that there can be no discrimination at all between men and women in the matter of remuneration. There are some kinds of work of which women may not be able to undertake. Men do work like loading, unloading, carrying and lifting heavier things, which women cannot do. In such cases there cannot be any discrimination it arises only where men and women doing the same or similar kind or work are paid differently. Wherever sex discrimination is alleged, there should be a proper job evaluation before any further enquiry is made. If the two jobs in an establishment are accorded an equal value by the application of those criteria which are themselves non-discriminatory (i.e., those criteria which look directly to the nature and extent of the demands made by the job) as distinct from criteria which set out different values for men and women on the same demand and it is found that a man and woman employed on these two jobs are paid differentially, then sex discretion clearly arises."

Women must fight back for their participation and respond to the demands of progress. Therefore, improvement of the status of women can be ensured only through their full integration and participation in the task of national development. Article 39(d) of the constitution proclaims equal pay for equal work for both men and women as a Directive Principles of State Policy, which has to be read into the fundamental rights as a matter of integration. Article 14 of the constitution enjoys the state not to deny any equality before the law or the equal protection of the laws and Article 16 declares that there shall be equal opportunity for all citizens in matters relating to employment or appoint to any office under the state. Section 2(b) of the equal Remuneration Act 1976 defines same work or similar nature to mean:[7]

"Work in respect of which the skill, efforts and responsibility required are the same when performed under similar working conditions, by a man or a woman and the differences, if any between the skill, effort and responsibility required of a man and those required of a woman are not of practical importance in relation to the terms and conditions of employment. In a leading case the Apex Court laid down the following tests to determine whether the work is same work or work of similar nature.

In India, women have remained backward owing to many factors through the scriptures laid down an exalted status for them. In recent years, there has been an increasing awareness and recognition of the fact that women who formed on half of the society cannot be ignored at all.

HARASSMENT OF WOMEN AT WORK

Council v/s A Chopra Harassment of the work place by the males is the reality of the workingwomen's life. Apex court upheld the removal of an employee from services of the Apparel Export Promotion Council on charges of sexual harassment, questioning an earlier verdict of the Delhi High Court. The Supreme Court observed that lenient in such cases was bound to have a demoralizing effect on workingwomen. [8]Basically the sexual harassment of a woman at the place of work is incompatible with the dignity and honor of a female and needs to be eliminated and that there can be no compromise with such violations admits of no debate.[9]

The harassments of women at work may manifest itself of follows:

(1) Action from sexual motives. This could be in the form of:

   (a) Demand of sexual forms for job benefits, and

   (b) Subjection of female employees to offensive environment polluted with verbal or physical abuses of sexual nature

(2) Acton that is based on an individual gender but are unrelated to sexual desires. This involves constant subjection of female employee to demanding treatment reinforcing sexual stereotypes, motivated by misogyny or chauvinism.

Self-consistent law is illusion. There should be consistent with all substantive and procedural law. In a similar vein, the IPC also give protection to this working class of women at work. Section 354 of IPC provides punishment for a person who assault or uses criminal force on any women intending or knowing is to be likely that he will thereby "outrage the modesty of a women" Section 509 of IPC prescribes punishment for a ward, gesture or act intended to outrage the industry of a women. In the present scenario the existing laws are not adequate in order to overcome problems pertaining to women generally. Moreover, there is lacuna while we implementing these laws. From the perspective of analyzing detail that the principle underlined under the *Vishaka V/s State of Rajasthan*[10] and rest of cases pronounced by the Apex Court are not effectively implementing any more. Basically the employers must have a duty to provide a suitable working environment for women in the modern society otherwise it would virtually impossible to live as human being. Furthermore the intrinsic, instrumental, natural rights have been violated.

The possible solution can be found in order to overcome sexual harassment in the working place. Firstly, certain and detailed company policy regarding sexual and gender bound harassment should be adopted and such policy must be well publicized. Secondly, an instutionalized but formal complaint procedure should be set up with high-ranking female officials to hear complaints. Thirdly, secrecy must be ensured to the victim. Fourthly, the special investigative agency must exist compromising both male and female officials to investigate complaint. Secondly appropriate disciplinary action must be taken against the offender. Last but not least, immediate action must be taken on every complaint in this regard.

MATERNITY BENEFITS

According to the Maternity Benefit (Amendment) Act, 1988 a women worker who has put in not less than 80 days work in the establishment can claim the following benefits from the employer:

(a) Maternity benefit at the rate of the average daily wage for the period of her actual absence, that is to say, the period immediately proceeds the day of her delivery and any period immediately following that day. The maximum period for which any woman shall be entitled to maternity benefit shall be twelve week of which not more than six weeks shall precede the date of her expected delivery.

(b) Medical bonus of Rs. 250 of no pre-natal confinement and post-natal confinement and post-natal care is provided for the employee free of charge.

(c) In case of miscarriage, a woman shall be entitled leave with wages at the rate of maternity benefit, for a period of six weeks immediately following the day of her miscarriage.

(d) In case illness arising out of pregnancy, delivery, premature birth of a child or miscarriage, in addition to the period of absence specified in (a) and (b) above, as the case may be, leave with wages at the rate of maternity benefit for a maximum period of one month.

(e) In case where a woman, having delivered a child dies during her delivery or during the period immediately following the date of her delivery for which she is entitled for the maternity benefit, leaving behind in either case and child, the employer shall be liable to pay maternity benefit for that entire period but if the child also dies during the said period, then for the days up to and including the date of death of the child.

Women constitute half the world's population, perform nearly two thirds of its work hours, receive one-tenth of the world's income and less than one hundreds of the world property.[11] The tremendous changes in industrialization, economic development are have enormous interests. Due to these rapid development women has got better protection under the Maternity Benefit Act. Maternity is a state of disability in a women worker from undertaking any work during the few work immediately proceeding and following childbirth. In order to protect the health of mother and child is in very much necessary. At the time when the International Labour Organization adopted the maternity protection convention in 1919[12] it was suggested that the countries represented should carry out inquiries into the question of maternity, benefits for women workers. The first central enactment in the sphere was the Mines Maternity Benefit Act 1941[13] later, the Employees State Insurance Act 1948 and the Plantation Labour Act 1951 passed also for the payment of maternity benefit. In 1961 the Central Maternity Benefit Act was passed aiming at a uniform maternity benefit all over the country.

In order to improve women's position in industry following measures would have to be incorporated in the industrial policies: Firstly changes in Education, which would enable women to improve their positions industrial employment, and to acquire transferable skills through various forms of vocational and informal training; Secondly, legal arrangements covering all aspects of industrialization from investment codes to regulations, which would provide for better general treatment of labor in industry; Thirdly, execution of employment opportunities in accordance with human resources development policies is essential; Fourthly, adoption of technology, which ensure stability of employment and professional progress to women workers. Fifthly, establishment of overall social central and of schemes for genuine workers participation in management and decision-making; lastly but not least, strengthening of self-reliance in industrial policies through industrial co-operation. The subject of women has received considerable attention in the last three decades. In the 1960 and early 1970, much of the Contribution came from feminists offering a critique of the and concentricity of empirical studies conducted by sociologists and economists which purported to describe the employment experience of all, while in fact they only addressed the experiences of men. Women represented by trade unions enjoy better pay and conditions on the whole than those who are not. Moreover, where trade unions are weak or nonexistent, women's work is more likely to be defined as unskilled or semi skilled.

According to section 46(1) Employees State Insurance Act 1948 focus to the insured persons or as the case may be, their dependants shall be entitled to the following benefits namely:

"Periodical payments to an insured woman in case of confinement or miscarriage or sickness arising out of miscarriage, such women being certified to be eligible for such payments by an authority specified in this hereby by the regulations". In the present scenario the statutory provisions in this regard are not being comfortably implemented. There is a lacuna in implementing the specific provisions of this Act. In view of this there must be judicial activism in order to eliminate the drawback or facets in the provision of the law without which it would virtually impossible to provide all facilities to the vulnerable classes of people like women.

REGIONAL AND INTERNATIONAL INSTRUMENTS OF INTERNATIONAL LABOR LAW

At the European level, a number of regional organizations that were created after the end of World War II have adopted legal instruments on labour matters. In the America, only few of the recently established regional organizations have adopted labour law instruments. The North American Free Trade Area (NAFTA) has the North American Agreement on Labor Cooperation, and the Caribbean Community and Common Market (CARICOM) has an Agreement on Social Security. However, the instruments of the Organization of American States (OAS) are still the main source of international labour law in the region. In Asia, none of the regional organizations has adopted legal instruments on labour matters–there are only recommendations, declarations and programmes dealing with these issues. In Africa, both of the recently established regional organizations, the Southern African Development Community (SADC) and the Common Market of Eastern and Southern Africa (COMESA), have human rights matters contained in their treaties. The UN General Assembly has adopted also a number of legally binding Conventions concerning labour matters. The most important ones are the Convention on the Elimination of all Forms of Racial Discrimination (1969), Elimination of all Forms of Discrimination against Women (1979), Right of the Child (1989), Status of the Refugees (1954) and Status of Stateless Person (1960). A number of provisions concerning labour matters are contained in the International Covenant on Economic, Social and Cultural Rights and the International Covenant on Civil and Political Rights, which are legally binding human rights agreements. Both were adopted in 1966 and entered into force 10 years later, making many of the provisions of the Universal Declaration of Human Rights effectively binding. Establishes the right of all workers and employers to form and join organizations of their own choice without prior authorization, and lays down a series of guarantees for the free functioning of organizations without interference by the public authorities. In December 1997, 121 countries had ratified this convention. Apart from these instrumental or intrinsic rights following are the specific conventions.

1. Right to Organize and Collective Bargaining Convention, 1949.
2. Forced Labour Convention, 1930.
3. Abolition of Forced Labour Convention, 1957.
4. Discrimination (Employment and Occupation) Convention 1958.
5. Equal Remuneration Convention, 1951.
6. Minimum Age Convention, 1973.

CONCLUSIONS

We can find out positive and effective contribution of the legislature in protecting the interest of women worker through legislative process. The present penal provisions in labor legislations are instrument to deter the employer. The machinery for inspection is also inadequate. A bare study or survey, however, brings out the hard reality that status of women and their status in the industries are not comfortable. But things are not so simple. Even if women do gain access to decision-making, and establish a presence as women over decisions, how do we know that they are acting in the interests of women as a social group which forces gender oppression? Further a survey of the working of Maternity Benefit Act reveals that instances are not lacking where women worker do not assert their right for fear of losing jobs. From the perspective of the equal remuneration for both sexes the Equal Remuneration Act, 1976, which prohibits discrimination between men and women in regard to wages, has not been effectively implemented even in organized sector. There should be effective implementation of the Maternity Benefit Act 1961 in all the states. Review of the existing laws is more concern of the society. Even if it is not possible there ought be amendment to the existing labour laws like Factories Act 1948, Employees State Insurance Act 1948, Maternity Benefit Act 1961 etc. Convening new laws or general guidelines are having enormous implications. Legal awareness to the working women through participation of NGO's local institutions and political bodies are required in order to strengthen the rights of women in the industrial or working sectors. It is suggested that a comprehensive legislation providing protection to female workers employed in the different industrial establishments should be enacted so that legislate rights are duly protected.

Notes

1. Section 27, Factories Act 1948
2. Section 14, Beedi and Cigar Workers Act 1966; GB Pai , *Labor Law in India*, Butterworth, New Delhi, p. 596-601.
3. AIR 197 Bom 27.
4. Mine Act 1952.
5. Dr. Justice A S Anand, *Justice for Women*, (Universal Law Publishing Co Pvt. Ltd.), 2002 Edition, p. 17.
6. 1987 Lab I.C. 961 (SC)
7. *Ibid;* See Namit Aggraval, *Women and Law in India*, (Central University, New Delhi, New Century Publication, p. 131.
8. AIR 1999 S 627.
9. 1980 UN Report; See *supra note* 5, p. 17.
10. SCC41 1997: 1997 SCC CRI(932)
11. UN Report 1980.
12. Krishna Ahooja Patel, 'Women in the working world an international Perspective', *Samya Shakti Journal of Women Studies*, Center for Women Development Studies, Vol. 2, No. 1, 1985, p. 1 at 3.
13. Malik, Industrial Law, Estern Book Company, 18th Edition, Eastern Book Company, Lucknow, p. 1734.

A Study of Issues and Violence on Dual Role of Working Women in Chennai City

R. Balasubramaniyan* & V. Priya**

"If you want to awaken country first awake women; if a woman is awakened, a family is awakened and a family is awakened, a village is awakened, thereby, entire country is awakened." — **Pundit Jawaharlal Nehru**

I

INTRODUCTION

M. K. Gandhi has stated that women are the noblest of God's creation, supreme in their own sphere of activity. The process of economic development would be incomplete and lopsided unless women are fully involved in it. Emancipation of women is an essential prerequisite for economic development and social progress of the nation. Economic empowerment of women has emerged has an important issue in our society in recent times. In India, despite enactments of several socio-economic legislations and the Indian Constitution declaring gender equality, the patriarchal values and normative structure established some two thousands years ago hindered women's emancipation and empowerment. The economic empowerment of women is of paramount importance to political thinkers, social scientists, women activists, politicians, legal luminaries, academicians and administrators. The total population of India was at 0.00 hours as on March 1, 2001, stood at 1,027,015,247 persons. With this, India stands in the second place after China to cross the one billion mark in population. The population of the country rose by 21.34 per cent during

* *Associate Professor, Department of Economics, D. G. Vaishnav College, Arumbakkam, Chennai, E-mail: baladgv@yahoo.co.in*

** *Research Scholar (2006-2007) in Economics, Centre for Distance Education, Bharathidasan University, Thiruchirappalli.*

1991-2001. In 1991, the total women population was 403 million and increased to 495 million in 2001, this would likely to go up to 615 million in 2016.

Women have been the backbone of Indian society, who are shouldering multifarious responsibilities in household chores and intending upbringing of children. The women from the landless households hire out their personal labour on the fields, sweating lower wages to supplement household earnings. Women always do household works like cooking, cleaning, washing cloths, child care, home maker management and educating the children, etc. According to the World Bank study (2008), normal housewives perform continuously on an average 8 hours of domestic chores and at the same time get nothing for their work. Presently, women produce 50 per cent of the world's food supply, account for 60 per cent of working force and contribute about 40 per cent of world's income, but receive only 10 per cent of the world's income and more surprisingly own less than 1 per cent of world's property. Women in agricultural households are greatly distressed. Agriculture is the dominant sector in India in terms of livelihood and the rural sector that houses the agriculture accounts for 60 per cent of India's population. While men move (migrate) to towns for earning, women suffer immobility due to household's responsibilities and lack of women living facilities in towns. This possibly creates a relative abundance of female labour in rural markets. Women are hired for arduous, injurious and monotonous work and command discriminatingly lower wage rates (Nilabja Ghosh, 2008).

Violence on women is of many types and dimensions. They are domestic, marital, occupational, private and public, religious and cultural, institutional and caste violence, etc. Everyday, in India on an average about 25 per cent women are subjected to domestic and public violence. Of which, 2 per cent of the women are committing suicides, 2 per cent are mentally retarded and 3 per cent are emotionally critical. Occupational violence such as exploitation, sexual harassment, scolding by the employer and discrimination poses a serious threat to women and family members of their existence. Employed women are facing day in and day out, emotions, job burdens, male chauvinistic burst and jaundiced environment. Emotional incompatibility with husband, in-laws and relatives, explosive habits of men at work place and antagonistic attitudes, generation gap and gender discrimination create role conflicts on women even now and then. In general, women are positioned themselves to pay the price for the benefits of economic independence, equal status and position of self-respect. Life and living are hard, especially in these days of limited opportunities and stiff competition. Women find themselves in a spot of bother because they are often losers in a competition for occupation, raw materials, capital, resources, investment, family support, and rest and recreation. A significant proportion of women are forced with pregnancy and motherhood without having any freedom to express their thoughts. This leads to health weakness and anemia of women. The rest of the paper is organized as follows. Section II explores the review of literature. Section III specifies the objectives and methodology of the study. Section IV underscores the results and discussion. Section V presents the major findings of the study and finally, section VI provides the conclusion.

II

REVIEW OF LITERATURE

Research studies on women issues and violence are in abundance both at micro and macro levels. Women employees can be grouped into three categories. The first group consists of women with educational, technical and professional qualifications manage with professional jobs. The second group of women constitutes those who do not possess any formal education and training, but having certain hereditary skills and courage's required setting up of small businesses which are developed practically. The third group of women who work in cities with lower means of livelihood and belongs to economically backward sections. Increasing affluence in agrarian families or increase in male earning is associated with women's withdrawal from the labour market and reduced labour supply (Bardhan, 1978; Dasgupta and Goldar, 2005), also inevitably increasing dependence and social subjugation. Unhappily, there is an apprehension that economic growth can lead to 'intensification of gender bias' (Dreze and Sen, 2003). There are evidences that women suffer more deprivation and food insecurity than the men who are deemed as bread winners. Yet research has also shown that women earnings can be more beneficial for the nutrition and health of the children (Kumar, 1978: Gulati, 1978) as men tend to spend on personal consumption such as alcohol and chewing tobacco.

Many studies have identified education, work participation, experience, cadre of job and exposure to outside living conditions as determinants for women economic status. Education enhances a women's position through decision making autonomy, control over resources, knowledge and work culture (Jejeebhoy, 1996 and Kishor, et al., 2004). Women's gainful employment outside home exposes her to the outside world; delays age at marriage, provide a sense of financial independence and increase her bargaining power and autonomy within the household and society (Chen, 1995). Also, women's paid employment could alter the perception of women's value and motivate investment in the girl child's education and health (United Nations). Women are often subjected to the dual role and burden of earning for the family and caring for the children and they are also often excluded from education, and decision making process in the family. It is evident from the empirical research that education discrimination against women hinders the process of economic development.

Atrocities, violence and discrimination are the three major problems, which the Indian women face in the present day society. The traditional mentalities of India assume that the place of women is mainly concentrated to the household activities like kitchen work and upbringing of the children. They have been considered as the sex object and inferior to men in different spheres of knowledge. The 'Sati Pratha', Pardha System, Child Marriage and Dowry System, etc., have been the major atrocities and discriminatory attitudes against women in India (Ramaswamy, 2006). Farm women are characterized by drudgery occupational hazard, low productivity and low income, which lead to poor diet, poor health and poverty. In the informal sector especially in beedi rolling, women often have to work very long hours to earn an income which is always low and this in turn affects the family and children. The root of cause of women being treated as second class citizens in an economy lies in the very status assigned to women within economic theory per se (Crystal David John, 2009). Pitt and Shahidur (1998) found that credit programmes provide larger benefits to poor households, when programme participants are women than men. Their estimates show that every 100 taka (Bangladesh currency) borrowed by women increases household expenditure by 18 taka compared to 11 taka for men.

Compared to their counterparts elsewhere in the country, women in Kerala have a better status due to high literacy rate, low morbidity rate, low drop outs rate of girls in school, better education and health facilities. Kerala is the first state where local bodies are advised to allocate 10 per cent of the developments funds for schemes directly targeting women. As a consequence of these measures women experienced some improvement in social fields, but still they do not have social, political, and economic entitlements that men possess (Dreze and Sen, 2002). Several studies brought out clearly that women's well being has a positive impact on family's well being also. Independent earnings of women enhance her social standing in the household and society (Sen, 1999). Reducing gender inequality in the labour market will increase women's economic security and contribute to economic development and growth. Empowerment of women is the process by which women acquire due recognition on par with men, to participate in the course of action of the society through the political and cultural institutions as a partner with human dignity (Ramaswamy, 2006). Human well being will be enhanced when women and men share equally with respect to social, economic, political and legal rights.

III

OBJECTIVES OF THE STUDY

1. To study the socio-economic characteristics of dual working women in Chennai city.
2. To identify the time use pattern of dual working women.
3. To examine the multifarious issues and violence concerning selected dual working women in Chennai city.

4. To analyze the health status of selected working women.
5. To suggest appropriate policy issues to overcome the problems and challenges of working women.

METHODOLOGY OF THE STUDY

The study is based on primary data. The primary data is collected through the well tested structured questionnaire and personally interviewed by the researcher in the chosen study areas in Chennai city. There are ten zones comes under the purview of corporation of Chennai city. Of which, Chennai Central was chosen for eliciting information's from the selected respondents. In Chennai Central, Saidapet, T. Nagar, Thousand lights, Mount Road and Triplicane are selected for the study. In each area by using random technique, 30 dual working women are selected. Thus, totally 150 respondents are selected for seeking information's relating to the dual working women in Chennai city. The working woman consists of multifaceted personalities hailing from different social, economic, religious and cultural backgrounds. They are school teachers, office goers, nurses working in private hospitals and bank clerks. Working women performs a dual role like the God Arthanareeswara, who possess the characteristics of both male and female. It represents the theory that men and women have each other's features, traits and tastes. But working women faces lot of obstacles and threats in the family and society. This study is primarily undertaken to unravel the mysteries behind the life of dual working women. Dual role is defined as the working woman performs two jobs in a day, one at home and the other at office. To make the study more meaningful and comparative, percentage and ratio analysis have been attempted in this study. The Chi-Square Test has been used in this study. Finally, the study was conducted during May-July 2007.

IV

RESULTS AND DISCUSSION

Table 1 presents the respondents age, educational attainment and marital status. Demographically, the age structure is considered to be important as it lays the foundation for creation of productive capacity of the individuals. Similarly, educational levels are taken as an important variable to gauge the relationship between education levels of the respondents and women employment. Marital status of the respondents is also considered a variable in determining the relationship between the marital status and dual role of working women. The table 1 reveals that about 33 per cent of working women are in the age group of 20-25, followed by 21 per cent in the age group of 25-30 and about 18 per cent belongs to the age group of 30-35. This suggests that younger the age more will be the participation rates of working women. The educational levels of the respondents indicate that about 46.7 per cent attained degree level qualification, followed by 20 per cent with below degree level and about 17 per cent obtained P.G. Degrees. The marital status of the respondents reveals that about 60 per cent of the working women are married. Hence, there is a high positive correlation between age, education and marital status of the respondents.

Table 1
Age, Education and Marital Status of the Respondents

Age Group	*Number of working women*	*Percentage*
20-25	50	33.3
25-30	32	21.3
30-35	27	18.0
35-40	22	14.7
40 & above	19	12.7
Total	150	100
Education Qualification		
Less than Degree Level	30	20.0
Degree Level	70	46.7
P.G. Degree Level	26	17.3
Technical/Professional Level	24	16.0
Total	150	100
Marital Status		
Married	90	60.0
Unmarried	48	32.0
Divorcees	8	5.3
Widow	4	2.7
Total	150	100

Source: Primary Survey.

Table 2 captures the type of family and family size of the respondents in Chennai city. The type of family nucleus or joint influences the working women's responsibility in playing a dual role. A joint family sometimes protects the interest of a working woman but on more occasions, it gives a woman to shoulder heavy responsibility at home. On the other hand, a nucleus family seems to eases the burden of working woman in general, but caring and educating the children is not that easy for a working woman. In our study, about 62 per cent of the dual working women belong to nuclear family and only 38 per cent comes under the joint family. The family size of the respondents is an important variable in gauging the degree of responsibility of the working women in both at home and office. About 48 per cent of the respondents are having small family (up to 2 children) followed by medium family (up to 4 children) and large family ,(more than 4 children). These suggest that smaller the family, lesser will be the relative responsibility of the working women.

Table 2
Type of Family and Family Size of the Respondents

Description/Type	*Frequency*	*Percentage*
Joint	57	38
Nuclear	93	62
Total	150	100
Family Size		
Small	72	48
Medium	61	41
Large	17	11
Total	150	100

Source: Primary Survey.

Table 3 provides the income and expenditure pattern of the respondents. It reveals that about 41 per cent of the respondents earning monthly income of below Rs. 7500, followed by 33 per cent earn income in the range of Rs. 7501-12500 and about 26 per cent earns income of above Rs. 12500. The expenditure pattern of the respondents shows mixed results. About 48 per cent of the respondents spent income in the range of Rs. 5001-10000 per month, followed by 28 per cent spends above Rs. 10000 and only 24 per cent spend below Rs. 5000. These suggest that there is some correlation between income and expenditure pattern of the respondents in the study area. The Keynesian theory points out that there is a positive correlation between income and consumption of an individual. The size of expenditure of dual working women varies from time to time. As income increases, the family expenditure tends to increase for obvious reasons. As one should keep an eye on the quantum of family expenditure, otherwise, it would lead towards debt trap.

Table 3
Income and Expenditure Pattern of the Respondents

Monthly Income in Rs	*Frequency*	*Percentage*
Below 7500	62	41
7501-12500	49	33
Above 12500	39	26
Total	150	100
Monthly Expenditure in Rs.		
Below 5000	36	24
5001-10000	72	48
Above 10000	42	28
Total	150	100

Source: Primary Survey.

Table 4 shows the types of health problem faced by the dual working women in Chennai city. Health is one the indicators of human development.

Indian dual working women are facing multiple health related problems on account of obvious reasons. Occupational health hazards are one of the emerging issues in developing countries. Occupational and family stress is the major cause for concern in the study area. It reveals that majority of the respondents are having health related problems. About 28 per cent of dual working women are having severe spinal problems in the study area, followed by 23 per cent thyroid, 18 per cent head ache, 15 per cent digestive problems, 11 per cent blood pressures and 5 per cent affected with anemic and T.B. These reveal the fact that dual role and responsibility of working women in Chennai city causing multiple health related problems. The major reasons for health problems of dual working women are: long hours of work, long hours of sitting or standing in the office or at home, untimely consumption of food, mental stress, discrimination of work load, more time spent in household work, lack of rest, abnormal behaviors of husband and family members, etc. Evidence from this study suggests that many women repent for having to carry a dual workload both in the office and at home. Because most of the working women are unable to attend to the guests and social gatherings, feeling guilty towards giving low motherly care to the children and lack of time to spend in caring aged people at home.

Table 4
Type of Health Problems of the Respondents

	Yes		*No*		*Total*	
Type of Health Problem	*Count*	*Percentage*	*Count*	*Percentage*	*Count*	*Percentage*
Anemic	7	5	143	95	150	100
Back Pain	41	28	109	72	150	100
Skin Problem	15	10	135	90	150	100
Head ache	27	18	123	82	150	100
Digestive problem	23	15	127	85	150	100
Blood pressure	16	11	134	89	150	100
Thyroid	34	23	116	77	150	100
Diabetes	6	4	144	96	150	100
T.B.	7	5	143	95	150	100

Source: Primary Survey.

Table 5 presents the time use pattern of the respondents. In economic theory, time spent by the labourers at work spot is considered as one of the important variable in measuring the productivity of the workers. In our study, time pattern of the respondents is taken as an important variable in gauging the relationship between dual role of working women and plausible health related problems. It shows that household work, children care, and shopping constitute the core in which working women are spending below 2 hours per day. On an average, about 33 working women spends up to 4 hours household work and 50 working women spends time with children for about 3-4 hours every day. Time taken out for travel also constitutes an important variable in influencing women health related problems. In our study, about 150 women workers spend time below 2 hours for traveling to attend office duties. Sleeping is an important variable considered for examining the robustness of health of working women. About 100 working women sleep well with 7-8 hours per day. But the cause for concern belongs to 50 working women who on an average sleep less than 5-6 hours per day. This postulates the Becker theory on human capital which states that the variable, low rest or poor sleeping especially for dual working women across the globe generally affects their health system. The working woman spends about 7-8 hours in the office which is considered normal by ILO yardsticks. But most of the respondents out of fear of punishment or disciplinary action by the employers concealed the fact that normally on an average women employees work for about 9-10 hours. Hence, higher workload coupled with long hours of sitting or standing and significant domestic works resulting in dual working women having larger health problems in Chennai city.

Table 5
Time Use Pattern of the Respondents

Type of Activities per Day	*Below 2 hours*	*3-4 hours*	*5-6 hours*	*7-8 hours*	*Total*
Household work	117	33	-	-	150
Travel	150	-	-	-	150
Office	-	-	-	150	150
Children care	100	50	-	-	150
Sleeping	-	-	50	100	150
Shopping	150	-	-	-	150
Leisure time	150	-	-	-	150

Source: Primary Survey.

Table 6 pinpoints the egocentric reasons of the respondents in the study area. There are many types of egocentric reasons and primarily most of the reasons are positive to the women's empowerment. There are five major egocentric reasons are being considered in this study. Among the egocentric reasons considered, to become 'economically independent' is emerged as an important factor for dual working women employees' empowerment. Out of

Table 6
Respondents Egocentric Reasons

Egocentric Reasons	*Frequency*	*Percentage*
To become socially independent	34	23
To become economically independent	65	43
To be self reliant	25	17
To acquire skills	16	10
To become rich	10	7
Total	150	100

Source: Primary Survey.

150 respondents considered for the study, about 65 (43 per cent) women workers opined that their income carning capacity through employment makes them as 'economically independent'. About 23 per cent of the samples considered to become socially independent, the other egocentric variables such as self dependency, skill acquirements and to be rich posted an insignificant response from the dual working women employees. There are studies in economic literature which has taken up egocentric consumer behavior as one of the indispensable factor in forging a relationship between the quantity demanded and price of a product. Similarly, there are many women's studies in India examined the egocentric behaviors of women workers.

Table 7 examines the core of the study, namely, types of violence on dual working women in Chennai city. The violence against women and on women is not of recent origin. It is there ever since men and women were born in this planet. There are many types of violence on women such as domestic violence, violence at work place, emotional violence, institutional violence, political violence and cultural violence. In our study, we considered the domestic and violence at work place on women employees are the main variables to estimate the quantum of violence on dual working women. Domestic violence on women workers accounted for 28 per cent, followed by assaults by husbands (20 per cent), dowry issues (18 per cent) and in-laws bricking (10 per cent). These suggest that working women are subjected to unleashed violence at home. The official (work spot) violence on women workers are not only dangerous but also pose a big threat on the existence of women in general. There is increasing violence on women workers at work spot. Our study reveals that ill-treatment of women workers is the serious factor which accounted for 23 per cent, followed by fellow male chauvinisms (15 per cent) and sexual harassments (11 per cent). Most of the violence on women is not reported to the police personnel's for obvious reasons. Basically, the fear of outraging the modesty of women by the men haunting the womenfolk's in general. Hence, the violence on dual working women is the most critical factor and which is unabated not only in Chennai city but also across the globe.

Table 7
Types of Violence on Dual Working Women

	Yes		*No*		*Total*	
Type of Violence	*Count*	*Percentage*	*Count*	*Percentage*	*Count*	*Percentage*
Domestic Violence	41	28	109	72	150	100
Assaulted by husbands	30	20	120	80	150	100
Dowry menace	27	18	123	82	150	100
In-laws bricking	15	10	135	90	150	100
Male Chauvinism	23	15	127	85	150	100
Sexual harassments at office	16	11	134	89	150	100
ill-Treatment of women workers	34	23	116	77	150	100

Source: Primary Survey.

Hypothesis-I

Null Hypothesis: There is no association between the women workers and domestic violence.

Table 8
Chi-Square Test for Association between the Women Workers and Domestic Violence

	Women workers Yes		*Women workers No*		*Total*		
Type of Violence	*Count*	*Percentage*	*Count*	*Percentage*	*Count*	*Chi Square value*	*P Value*
Domestic Violence	41	28	109	72	150	4.156	0.002
Assaulted by husbands	30	20	120	80	150		
Dowry menace	27	18	123	82	150		

Table 8 examines the hypothesis-I which states that there is no association between women workers and domestic violence. The quantum of violence on working women unleashed by their family members especially husbands and in-laws are very significant in the context of domestic violence which is unabated in India. In our study, domestic violence, assaults on women by the husbands and Dowry menace have emerged as the significant factors responsible for violence on women workers. The Chi-Square test is used to test the co-relation between the chosen respondents and the degree of domestic violence they encountered at home. Since the P value is less than 0.05, the null hypothesis is rejected at 5 per cent level of significance. Hence, there is an association between women workers and domestic violence unleashed on them in the study area.

Hypothesis-II

Null Hypothesis: There is no association between the women workers and violence at Work Spot.

Table 9
Chi-Square Test for Association between the Women Workers and Violence at Work Spot

	Women workers Yes		*Women workers No*		*Total*		
Type of Violence	*Count*	*Percentage*	*Count*	*Percentage*	*Count*	*Chi Square value*	*P Value*
ill-Treatment of women workers	34	23	116	77	150	2.282	0.001
Male Chauvinism	23	15	127	85	150		
Sexual harassments at office	16	11	134	89	150		

Table 9 underscores the hypothesis-II which states that there is no relationship between the women workers and violence at work spot. There is an increasing violence on women workers at work spot. Our study reveals that ill-treatment of women workers is the serious factor which accounted for 23 per cent, followed by fellow male chauvinisms (15 per cent) and sexual harassments (11 per cent). To test the co-relation between the respondents and quantum of violence on them at work spot, Chi-Square test has been used. Since the P value is less than 0.05, the null hypothesis is rejected at 5 per cent level of significance. Hence, there is an association between women workers and work spot violence which is quite significant on them. Hence, the work spot environment is not conducive for women employees to perform their jobs without fear and stress.

V

MAJOR FINDINGS OF THE STUDY

1. The study reveals that about 33 per cent of working women are in the age group of 20-25, followed by 21 per cent in the age group of 25-30 and about 18 per cent belongs to the age group of 30-35. This suggests that younger the age more will be the participation rates of working women.
2. The educational levels of the respondents indicate that about 46.7 per cent attained degree level qualification, followed by 20 percent with below degree level and about 17 per cent obtained P.G. Degrees. The marital status of the respondents reveals that about 60 per cent of the working women are married. Hence, there is a high positive correlation between age, education and marital status of the respondents.
3. The family size of the respondents is an important variable in gauging the degree of responsibility of the working women in both at home and office. About 48 per cent of the respondents are having small family (up to 2 children) followed by medium family (up to 4 children) and large family (more than 4 children). These suggest that smaller the family, lesser will be the relative responsibility of the working women.
4. The size of expenditure of dual working women varies from time to time. As income increases, the family expenditure tends to increase for obvious reasons. As one should keep an eye on the quantum of family expenditure, otherwise, it would lead towards debt trap.
5. The most of the respondents out of fear of punishment or disciplinary action by the employers concealed the fact that normally on an average women employees work for about 9-10 hours per day. Hence, higher workload coupled with long hours of sitting or standing and significant domestic works resulting in dual working women having larger health problems in Chennai city.

6. Out of 150 respondents considered for the study, about 65 (43 per cent) women workers opined that their income earning capacity through employment makes them as 'economically independent'. About 23 per cent of the samples considered to become socially independent, the other egocentric variables such as self dependency, skill acquirements and to be rich posted an insignificant response from the dual working women employees.
7. In our study, we considered the domestic and violence at work place on women employees are the main variables to estimate the quantum of violence on dual working women. Domestic violence on women workers accounted for 28 per cent, followed by assaults by husbands (20 per cent), dowry issues (18 per cent) and in-laws bricking (10 per cent).
8. There is an increasing violence on women workers at work spot. Our study reveals that ill-treatment of women workers is the serious factor which accounted for 23 per cent, followed by fellow male chauvinisms (15 per cent) and sexual harassments (11 per cent). Most of the violence on women is not reported to the police personnel's for obvious reasons.
9. The Chi-Square test is used to test the co-relation between the chosen respondents and the degree of domestic violence they encountered at home. Since the P value is less than 0.05, the null hypothesis is rejected at 5 per cent level of significance. Hence, there is an association between women workers and domestic violence on them in the study area.
10. To test the co-relation between the respondents and quantum of violence on them at work spot, Chi-Square test has been used. Since the P value is less than 0.05, the null hypothesis is rejected at 5 per cent level of significance. Hence, there is an association between women workers and work spot violence which is quite significant on them.

VI

CONCLUSION

The present study is focused on the women workers issues and violence on them in Chennai city. Women's access to job may once have been a forbidden issue, but in today's highly competitive and tough economic environment, job is now an essential thing for most women. The employment has become absolutely necessary for a woman if she is to lead a decent and independent life. Women enters labour market with a view to earn income and support the family. Working women performs a dual role to sustain the family. A lot of women are still playing multiple roles as caregiver, home maker, spouse, mother to her children and employee without realizing that they are shouldering burden than they work normally. Most arguably the factors such as personal activities, spousal relationship, family and office responsibilities of an employed women and its intertwined role with the perception on marital issues could be a drawing reflection for future vindication of women empowerment. Another dimension to the women issues is the absence or lack of enforcement of social and labour legislation which hampers women's access to employment benefits. In many firms, women are denied rights such as maternity benefits, medical leave, crèche and legal aid. Changes in work pattern of are often accompanied by changes in marital and child rearing patterns. There is more overlap between private lives and work lives of a woman than is generally acknowledged.

The dual role of working women today is a necessary characteristic of modern society. Research studies on women issues and dual role are in abundance at the global level. Many studies have identified education, work participation, experience, cadre of job and exposure to outside living conditions as determinants for women economic status. In many countries, the increasing labour force participation of women in many economic activities means that the empowerment of women is natural rather than compulsion. Woman in India also suffer from bias against woman because of the cultural and traditional values. The expected behavioral pattern of woman which is marked by modesty and lack of articulation is often misinterpreted as incompetence and lack of professionalism. In this setting, the transition itself from a "non-professional" approach to a "professional" one is an extra effort for woman. In addition, woman by themselves find it difficult to interact and discuss such issues as equals, because they have been trained to listen, obey and leave decisions to men in the family. The condescending views of others do little to support them.

Policy Issues

(a) About 33 per cent reservation for women and 84th Constitution Amendment Bill should be passed in the parliament and it should become a law.

(b) Reducing gender inequality in the labour market will increase women's economic security.

(c) Work spot violence or domestic violence against the women in any form has to be abolished with strict vigilance.

(d) Education of women is a fundamental right and hence all girls between 6-14 years of age should be given free education with mid-day meals.

(e) Economic, social, political and holistic empowerment of women is a must to ensure women emancipation and progress in the society.

References

Balasubramaniyan, R. (2008), "A Study of the Status of Women Entrepreneurs and Determinants of their Empowerment in India", in Rathakrishnan, L. [Ed] Empowerment of Women through Women Entrepreneurship, Gyan Publishers, New Delhi, pp. 85-97.

Balasubramaniyan, R. (2009), "Management of Women Entrepreneurial Changes in Beauty Parlour Industry in Chennai City," Global Management Review, Salem, Vol. 3, Issue 3, May, pp. 48-57.

Cinamon, R. G. and Rich, Y. (2002), "Profiles of Attributions of importance to Life Roles and their Implications for the Work-Family Conflict", *Journal of Family Psychology*, Vol. 49(2), pp. 212-220.

Crowell, A. Nancy and Burgess (1996), "Understanding Violence against Women", National Research Council (ed), pp. 77-78.

Duxbury, L. E. and Higgins, C. A. (1991), "Gender Differences in Work-Family Conflict", *Journal of Applied Psychology*, Vol .76(1), pp. 60-73.

Fox, M.L. and Dwyer, D.J. (1999), "An Investigation of the Effects of Time and Involvement in the Relationship between Stressors and Work-Family Conflict", *Journal of Occupational Health Psychology*, Vol. 4(2), pp. 164-174.

Kapoor Pramila, (1971), "Marriage and Working Women in India", Vikas Publications, New Delhi.

Priya, V. (2007), "A Study of Dual Role of Working Women in Chennai City", An Unpublished M.Phil Dissertation submitted to the Bharathidasan University, Thiruchirappalli, pp. 1-68.

Renuka Devi, V. (2005a), "Legal Rights of Women Entrepreneurship in India", *Quantanomics Journal*, Chennai, pp. 5-12.

Renuka Devi, V. (2005b), "The Role of Indian Working Women and Socio-Economic Transformation," *Quantonomics Journal*, Chennai, pp. 13-18.

Soundari, S. M. H. and Sudhi, M. A. (2003), "Gender Disparity in Tamil Nadu", *Social Welfare*, Vol. 49(12), pp. 24-27.

Steven, J. (1988), "Gender Identity and Roll Conflict among Men and Women", *Journal of Psychology*, Vol. 122(6) pp. 567-576.

Domestic Violence in India– A Milestone in Protection of Women

RATTAN SINGH* & MEHAK AHUJA**

INTRODUCTION

Violence against women and girls is the most pervasive human rights violation in the world today. Opening the door on the subject of violence against the world's females is like standing at the threshold of an immense dark chamber vibrating with collective anguish, but with the sounds of protest throttled back to a murmur. Where there should be outrage aimed at an intolerable status quo there is instead denial, and the largely passive acceptance of 'the way things are.'[1]

We live in a democratic society where women constitute nearly one-half of the population. From times immemorial, a woman has not only denied justice, equality and liberty but she has also been socially, economically, physically, psychologically, emotionally as well as sexually exploited at home, in office and at everywhere and has been forced to lead an immoral and destitute life. Women are the best and the most beautiful creation of God on this cosmos and in our nation on one hand, women are worshipped and honoured as Goddesses of Laxmi, Saraswati, Parvati and Durga but on the other hand, they are considered as an object of contempt and ridicule, a commodity for barter, an expendable asset and a plaything for mere sexual enjoyment.[2] To consider her 'a weaker sex' is a big mistake as she has contributed and sacrificed not less than man in national movements, in the development of nation etc. and the best instances are with us of Rani Laxmi Bhai of Jhansi, Sarojini Naidu, Indira Gandhi, Pratibha Patil, Mother Teresa, P.T. Usha, Amrita Pritam, Kiran Bedi, Indira Nooyi, Kalpana Chawla, Sunita Williams, Saniya Mirza and lots of.

* *Professor, University Institute of Laws, Panjab University Regional Campus, Ludhiana, (Punjab).*

** *LL.M., Guru Nanak Dev University Amritsar (Punjab).*

The Constitution, is the supreme law of our nation, provides provisions for the protection of women against such exploitation but inspite of such stringent provisions it is ludicrous to say that- a woman is still unsafe. No doubt we live in 21st Century where the human civilization has developed a lot but exploitation, discrimination and violation against women is still on the heights and we find such barbarous incidents of violence daily here and there inception from the womb. Violence means unwarranted use of force or use of force against public liberty to cause injury, loss or damage.[3] It is manifested in the form of infanticide or foeticide and after birth she is greeted with hatred, silence and considered as a burden upon the family and then started the discrimination between a boy child and a girl child, less priority is given to her in giving love, affection, care, education and in all the other walks of life. The reality of the Indian families is that "boys are brought up to be served, girls to serve. Boys are princes in the family, girls' maids in the scullery."[4] Sexual harassment by the eve-teasers and at the working places, depreiving her from her economic resources, giving her verbal abuses, physical, psychological, emotional and mental pains etc. also constitute acts of violence.

The word 'domestic' origins from the Latin word means 'house'[5] and Violence against women shall be understood to encompass, but not limited to physical, including battering, sexual abuse of female children in the household, dowry related violence, marital rape, female genital mutilation and other traditional practices harmful women.[6] *According to the United Nations Declaration on the Elimination of Violence Against Women,* 'Violence against women means any act of gender-based violence that results in, or is likely to result in, physical, sexual or psychological harm or suffering to women, including threats of such acts, coercion or arbitrary deprivation of liberty, whether occurring in public or in private life.'

Thus, domestic violence connotes when such harsh, inhuman and atrocious acts of violence is being committed to a woman at home i.e. by the persons to whom she is related to marriage, consanguinity, adoption and with whom she is living in a home or we can say that behind the closed doors. In other words, it can be defined as the maltreatment by one person to the woman living in the same home. It is a major social problem largely prevalent in our society. It involves a situation where a strong and powerful person in a home takes advantage of his position and becomes violent towards the weaker one. It distorts the development of each member at home and also their closed relatives.

Violence taking place within the family sphere, or domestic violence, is revealed to be of the most difficult and complex kind to combat. There are several reasons for this, including the cultural acceptance of the right of husbands to beat their wives, the legal doctrine of non-interference into private life, the private/public divide and the sacrosanct nature of the family[7]. The other reason can be woman's hesitant nature and due to her nature she does not come forward and report the crime. She prefers to live separately and walk out of the marriage by arranging alternative economic resources. But we should remember that, "Without woman the beginning of our world would be helpless, the middle without pleasure and the end void of consolation."[8]

In order to curb the acts of violence against the women, the Parliament has enacted a law namely '*The Protection of Women from Domestic Violence Act, 2005* in 2005.

Before the enactment of this act, the violence against women is protected in the following provisions of the various laws-

Prior to this Act, cruelty against woman is covered under Section 498-A (husband or relatives of husband of a woman subjecting her to cruelty) of *Indian Penal Code, 1860* which does not include all aspects of domestic violence. Earlier it was the only weapon which women has for fighting cruelty against her and is found wanting.

Section 304-B (dowry death) of *Indian Penal Code, 1860* provides that a person is punishable only for dowry death. Section 306 (abetment to suicide), Section 354 (assault or criminal force to woman with intent to outrage her modesty), Section 509 (word gesture or act intended to insult the modesty of a woman), section 375 (rape), 376 (punishment for rape), 376-A (intercourse by a man with his wife during separation), 376-B (intercourse by public servant with woman in his custody), 376-C (intercourse by superintendent of jail, remand home, etc.), 376-D (intercourse by any member of the management or staff of a hospital with any woman in that hospital), 377 (unnatural offences), Section 363-A (kidnapping or maiming a minor for the purposes of begging), Section 364 (kidnapping or abducting in order to murder), Section 364-A (kidnapping for ransom), Section 366 (kidnapping, abducting or inducing woman to compel her marriage), Section 366-A (procuration of minor girl), Section 366-B (importation of girl from foreign country), Section 369 (kidnapping or abducting child under ten years with intent to steal from its person), Section 498 (enticing or taking away a married woman), Section 372 (selling minor for the purposes of prostitution), Section 373 (buying minor for the purposes of prostitution etc.) of *Indian Penal Code, 1860* are there to protect women from different types of violence.

Section 113-A (Presumption as to abetment of suicide by a married woman) and 113-B (Presumption as to Dowry Death) of the *Indian Evidence Act, 1872* provides that if a person has committed the dowry death of a woman and has been subjected by such person to cruelty or harassment for or in connection with any demand for dowry, the court shall presume that such person has caused the dowry death.

The Muslim Women (Protection of Rights on Divorce) Act, 1986 has been specially enacted to protect the rights of Muslim women who have been divorced by or have obtained divorce from their husbands.

The Indecent Representation of Women (Prohibition) Act, 1986 was passed to restrict the indecent representation of women through advertisements or in publications, writings, paintings, figures, drawings, slides, photographs, films and if any individual does so shall be punishable with a minimum sentence of 2 years.

Dowry is a deep social rooted problem which is a big hindrance in the development of our society. It started as a custom to give presents to girl on her marriage but with the time and due to consistent rapacious demands by the cunning husbands and their relatives, it becomes a social evil resulting in dowry deaths and suicides. In order to curb this social evil, the legislature has enacted a law namely *'Dowry Prohibition Act, 1961'* which provides to receive and to give dowry both are offences and penalized.

Female infanticide and female foeticide are the other social evils that are widely prevalent in our nation. The main reasons for that are– immense love for the male child, evil of dowry, son is considered necessary to perform the rituals of the family, desire for a son as only son can survive the name of the ancestors, only he supports his old parents. But we are overlooking this thing that the females give birth to the males not males give birth to females. 'When the female (infant) buried alive she questioned for what crime she was killed...'[9] So in order to correct skewed sex ratio, the legislature has enacted a law namely *'The Pre-conception and Pre-natal Diagnostic Techniques (Prohibition of Sex Selection) Act, 1994'.*

Sati connotes burning or burying alive of the woman either forcibly or voluntarily along with her deceased husband's corpse. To combat this social evil the parliament has enacted a law namely *'The Commission of Sati Prevention Act, 1987'.* It not only prevents the commission of sati but also prevents its glorification.

Section 125 of *Criminal Procedure Code, 1973* protects right of legally wedded wives to get maintenance from their husbands. The right to maintenance under this section is a statutory right which the legislature has created and the said provision is independent of personal law or any other customary law governing the parties.[10] Section 24 of *Hindu Marriage Act, 1955* also empowers the court to grant maintenance *pendete lite* and other expenses to the wife or her children. Section 18 of *Hindu Adoptions and Maintenance Act, 1956* also provides that a hindu wife shall be entitled to maintenance by her husband during her lifetime but she is not entitled to separate residence and maintenance from her husband if she is unchaste or ceases to be a hindu by conversion to another religion.

Section 6 of *Hindu Succession Act, 1956* as amended in 2005 entitles a females will have the same rights as males to reside in, to claim partition and to inherit property. It will aid to those women who face violence or any kind of cruelty in their husband's home.

Under the *Family Courts Act, 1984*, the family courts have been established to provide a speedy and less expensive justice to the needy people facing matrimonial problems.

If the husband is violent and abusive, another legal remedy available is under the *Law of Torts*. Tort law deals with the liability of a person for wrongs committed against another including the wrong of 'trespass to the person'. Trespass to the person is the broad term used to denote various forms of physical and psychological injury committed upon a person- assault, battery and false imprisonment.[11]

The most significant movement for the protection of women is the adoption of *Convention on the Elimination of all kinds Discrimination Against Women* (CEDAW) by the United Nations General Assembly. In 1992, CEDAW formulated a broad recommendation that defined gender-based violence as a form of discrimination, placing it squarely within the rubric of human rights and fundamental freedoms and making clear that states are obliged to eliminate violence perpetrated by public authorities and by private persons.[12] And the problem of status of women has also been highlighted by observing 'International Women's Day.'

Another most significant movement to protect women from violence is in September 1995, the year of fiftieth anniversary of the founding of the United Nations, fourth World Conference on Women was held in Beijing known as *Beijing Declaration* for the protection of women against violence. It provides that: 'Violence against women both violates and impairs or nullifies the enjoyment by women of their human rights and fundamental freedoms. The long-standing failure to protect and promote those rights and freedoms in the case of violence against women is a matter of concern to all States and should be addressed.'[13]

Inspite of number of provisions as stated above, a woman is not protected. So there exists a need to enact a law which specifically provides protection to women from domestic violence which ensures the physical and mental safety of the women as well as to prevent them from being thrown out of the home.

THE PROTECTION OF WOMEN FROM DOMESTIC VIOLENCE ACT, 2005

The Domestic Violence Bill (Bill No. 116 of 2005) which had been pending before the Lok Sabha for many years has finally been given assent to by the President on 13th September, 2005 but came into force on October 26, 2006 as detailed consultations were required with the State and other agencies for framing the rules. There have been a number of changes made to it and serious lacunae that existed at the time and afterwards, the NDA government drafted it and suitably amended.

BASIC FEATURES OF THE ACT

'The Protection of Women from Domestic Violence Act, 2005' has been enacted to provide more effective protection to the rights of the women guaranteed under articles 14, 15 and 21 of the Constitution and to curb the barbarous acts of violence. This act is divided into five chapters and 37 sections. It is a comprehensive law and exhaustively includes all kinds of violence related to women and for the first time that an act has been made to include all kinds of women's violence in such detail. Union Law minister H.R. Bhardwaj told Parliament on Monday, 15th Dec. 2008 that Women in live-in relationships are also protected under the Domestic Violence Act. The basic features of this act are as follows:

1. *Protects women from a domestic relationship:* Domestic Relationship[14] means a relationship between two persons who live and have lived together at any point of time in a shared household[15] and are related by or through consanguinity, marriage, adoption or through joint family. It includes those women who are sisters, widows, mothers, daughters, single women or any woman residing with the abuser who is related to him in any way. Thus, this present act has enlarged the sphere to protect women from all their domestic relationships as prior to this they were protected by a relationship only through blood and marriage. In this way, the meaning of aggrieved person[16] also becomes wide.
2. *Broad meaning of respondent*[17]: In *Nand Kishore v. State of Rajasthan*[18], the Rajasthan High Court has held Section2 (q) and its proviso if read together nowhere suggests that relative of husband or male partner has to be a male. The word is relative not male relative and therefore, the female relative is not excluded from the definition of respondent.
3. *Protects women from domestic violence:* Domestic Violence[19] includes any act, omission, commission or conduct of the abuser that harms, injures, harasses or endangers the health, safety, life, limb or well-being whether mental or physical to the women. It includes actual violence as well as threat to give such violence. Further it includes physical abuse, sexual abuse, verbal and emotional abuse and economic abuse.
   (a) *Physical abuse:* It includes any kind of physical pain for instance:
      - Hitting, kicking, shoving, slapping, pushing, beating, punching, biting and jostling.
      - Assault, criminal intimidation and criminal force.

      Thus, it includes any kind of bodily pain, harm or injury that dangers to her life, limb or health and impairs the health and development.

   (b) *Sexual abuse:* It includes any kind of unwelcome sexually conduct or remarks for instance–

- Forcing to have a sexual intercourse.
- Forcing to look at pornography or at obscene or lascivious pictures or material.
- Forcing to entertain others.
- Any kind of physical contact.
- Sexually coloured remarks.

Thus, it includes any act of sexual nature that abuses, humiliates, dishonours, mortifies or degrades the dignity of the women.

(c) *Verbal and Emotional abuse:* It includes any kind of insulting or any kind of abasing, embarrassing, jeering remarks for instance–

- Name calling.
- Giving her demeaning, humiliating or undermining remarks or statement.
- Insulting or ridiculing her for not begetting a male child.
- Insulting or ridiculing her for not begetting any child.
- Harassing her for not bringing dowry or for not bringing sufficient dowry.
- Menacing her again and again to cause physical pains to any person in which she is interested.
- Forcing her to marry against her will.
- Preventing her to marry a person of her choice.
- Forcing her to marry a particular person of his/their choice.
- Threat to commit suicide.
- Any kind of allegations on her conduct and character.

(d) *Economic abuse:* It includes following:

- Depreiving her from her economic or financial resources such as stridhan or any property jointly owned by her with other person.
- Depreiving her from economic or financial resources of basic necessities such as not providing her food, shelter (forcing her to vacate a house or not to pay rent), clothes, medicines and other basic things.
- Refusing her to give maintenance.
- Preventing her from taking up a job or forcing her to leave a job.
- Disposal of household effects or any kind of alienation of assets whether movable or immovable, valuables, shares, securities, bonds, fixed deposits, jewellery or any property to which she is entitled or she has an interest or she requires for her or for her children by virtue of domestic relationship.

- Prohibiting or restricting her to continued access to resources, amenities, services or facilities to which she is entitled to use or enjoy by virtue of domestic relationship.

On October 28, 2006 police arrested a man at Melapalayam in Tirunelveli district of Tamil Nadu on a complaint of harassment from his wife only after a couple of days after the coming force of an act and perhaps it is the first case booked under the provisions of the protection of Women from Domestic Violence Act 2005 in the country.[20] Shashikala Mohite of Pune was granted maintenance of around Rs. 1000 in August, 2008 under the Protection of Women under Domestic Violence Act (PWDVA).[21]

4. *Provision of Protection Officers:* It provides for the appointment of protection officers in each district by the State government[22] to whom the aggrieved person or any person on his behalf report an act of domestic violence or its likelihood and the number of such officers may vary from district to district. His main duties and functions[23] are to assist the magistrate in discharging his functions, to ensure legal aid to the aggrieved person, to maintain a list of all service providers and shelter homes, to ensure the order providing monetary relief and to get the aggrieved person medically examined. He has to make a domestic incident report to the magistrate and forward copies to the police officer in charge of the local police station. He performs all his duties and functions under the control and supervision of Magistrate. No suit, prosecution or other legal proceedings shall be instituted against any protection officer for anything done in good faith.
5. *Punishment in case of non-compliance of duty:* It provides that if any protection officer fails or refuses to discharge his duties as directed by the Magistrate without any sufficient cause shall be punishable with imprisonment for a term which may extend to one year, or with fine which may extend to twenty thousand rupees, or with both.
6. *Protection Orders:* It provides that if magistrate is satisfied that any act of domestic violence has taken place or is likely to take place, then he is empowered to pass several Protection Orders[24] to protect the aggrieved person for instance he prohibits the abuser from committing, aiding or abetting any act of domestic violence to the aggrieved person and to any relative, dependants or any other person in which she is interested, restricts him from entering the premises where aggrieved person is employed or a school if she is a child or any place where she frequently visits, prohibits him to alienate any asset belonging to her or jointly held by her and restricts him to communicate in any form.
7. *Secures right of residence:* It provides for the rights of women to secure housing. It also provides for the right of a woman to reside in her matrimonial home or shared household, whether or not she has any

title or rights in such home or household[25]. This right is secured by a residence order[26], which is passed by the Magistrate.[27] He is empowered to pass a variety of residence orders for instance he can order the respondent to remove himself from the shared household, restraining him or any of his relatives from entering any portion of the house where the aggrieved person resides, restraining him from alienating or disposing of the shared household or from renouncing his right to the shared household, can impose any additional conditions, can order to execute a bond with or without sureties for preventing any act of domestic violence etc. He can also order him to pay rent or to secure the same level of alternative accommodation to the aggrieved person. In *S.R. Batra v. Taruna Batra*[28], the Supreme Court observed that the claim for alternative accommodation can only be made against the husband and not against the husband's in-laws or other relatives.

8. *Assistance by Service Providers:* It provides the provision of Service Providers[29] which are voluntary agencies or organizations which are established with the aim of protecting the rights and interests of women and providing them legal aid, medical, financial and other assistance. It has power to record the domestic incident report in a prescribed form and forward a copy to the Magistrate or to the protection officer, to get the aggrieved person medically examined and forward a copy of medical report to the protection officer and to provide her shelter in a shelter home. No suit, prosecution or other legal proceedings shall be instituted against any service provider or any member of it for anything done in good faith.
9. *Monetary Reliefs:* The Magistrate can order the respondent to pay Monetary Reliefs[30] to the aggrieved person which includes the expenses incurred resulting from domestic violence such as medical expenses, loss of earnings, loss of property and maintenance to the aggrieved person and to her children and damages for mental distress. The amount of monetary relief should be adequate, fair and reasonable and it can be either lump sum or monthly payment.
10. *Custody Orders:* No doubt there are many other laws relating to the custody of the children, but the Magistrate under this act is empowered to grant temporary custody of any child or children to the aggrieved person and makes arrangement so that the respondent may visit to meet them. But if any case any visit of the respondent may harm to the child or children then the Magistrate refuses him to visit.[31]
11. *Compensation Orders:* The Magistrate may pass any order, in addition to other reliefs, to direct the respondent to pay compensation and damages for the injuries including mental torture and emotional distress.[32]

12. *Provision for interim and ex-parte orders:* The Magistrate is empowered to grant any interim and ex-parte orders[33] on the satisfaction of the commission of any act of domestic violence. In *Bagadaram v. State of Rajasthan*[34], the Rajasthan High Court held that interim and ex-parte orders passed by the Magistrate under section 23 is appealable under section 29 and is not revisable under the provisions of Cr.P.C.
13. *Speedy trial and disposal:* It ensures speedy justice as it provides that the magistrate shall attempt to start proceedings and have the first hearing within 3 days of the complaint being filed in court and every case must be disposed of within a period of sixty days from the date of its first hearing.[35]
14. *Non-Bailable and cognizable:* A breach of protection order or interim protection order by the respondent is recognized as a cognizable and a non-bailable offence punishable with imprisonment for a term which may extend to one year, or with fine which may extend to twenty thousand rupees, or with both.
15. *Covers Legal Loophole:* A woman is subjected to cruelty by her husband or his relatives, it is an offence under *section 498-A* of the Indian Penal Code,1860. The civil law does not, however, address this phenomenon in its entirety and in order to protect the rights guaranteed under articles 14, 15 and 21 of Constitution and to provide a remedy under the civil law, this act has been enacted to protect the women from being the victims of domestic violence and to prevent the occurrence of domestic violence in the society.
16. *Aggrieved person can take services as well as can also file a complaint:* An important feature envisaged in this act that a woman who is the victim of domestic violence has the right to take the services of the police, shelter homes and medical establishments and simultaneously she also has the right to file her own complaint under Section 498-A of the Indian Penal Code,1860.
17. *More relief can be given:* This act ensures relief to a large number of harassed women as it covers all women including live-in relations.
18. Another important feature of this act is that it ensures that an aggrieved person, who takes recourse to the law, cannot be harassed for doing so.

DOMESTIC VIOLENCE IN OTHER COUNTRIES

MALAYSIA: N.G. Bernama of Kuala Lumpur, Malaysia on 3rd Dec. 2008 said that the government of Malaysia is currently reviewing its Domestic Violence Act, 1994 with the aim of expanding the scope of domestic violence.[36]

BULGARIA: Amendments to domestic violence act aim to improve assistance to Sofia Echo of Bulgaria, a working group, affiliated with the

Bulgarian Justice Ministry will prepare amendments to the Domestic Violence Prevention Act, the group's coordinator.[37]

BRAZIL: Inadequate government response to domestic violence occurs with striking regularity around the world. Domestic violence claims are frequently ignored, trivialized, and dismissed by police, by prosecutors and by judges. The situation in Brazil, like many other countries, is one in which domestic violence is against the law, but in practice is regularly tolerated. In Brazil, according to San Pablo Catholic University, only 2 per cent of criminal complaints for domestic violence against women lead to conviction of the aggressor.[38]

BRUNEI: Violence against women is a social ill in Brunei Darussalam that still needs to be dealt with, Pehin Orang Kaya Indera Pahlawan Dato Seri Setia Hj Suyoi Hj Osman, the Minister of Health delivered a speech, as the guest of honour at the Domestic Violence Symposium held in conjunction with the Asean Women's Day 2008. Pehin Dato Hj Suyoi stressed the need for a Domestic Violence Act to be introduced in Brunei to protect the rights of those who have been affected by domestic violence, similar to such acts introduced in neighbouring countries.[39]

BANGLADESH: There are two main laws relating to violence against women in Bangladesh: The Cruelty to Women (Deterrent Punishment) Ordinance (1983) and The Dowry Prohibition Act (1980). There are also articles in the Penal Code relating to rape. The Cruelty to Women Ordinance outlaws the kidnapping and abduction of women and acid throwing attacks on women, and mandates the death penalty or life imprisonment for causing the death of a rape victim. The same provisions apply to a husband and his family under the Dowry Prohibition Act, for the murder or attempted murder of a woman for dowry.[40]

Article 376 of the Penal Code mandates two years imprisonment, a fine, or both, for the rape of a woman by her husband. Article 342, however, requires that a woman undergo a medical examination immediately after rape, which in practice minimizes the possibility of a conviction being made. In any legal case, including cases of violence against women, if the complainant is absent, the case can be dismissed. In practice this discriminates against women who may be intimidated by their husbands or in-laws into staying away from court. In practice, convictions for rape and other violent crimes against women are rarely made, because women are unaware of their legal rights, because legal institutions are male-dominated and often inaccessible or unsympathetic to women, because of the difficulties of proving the case, because of legal loopholes, and because of an underlying undervaluation of women.[41]

PAKISTAN: Issues relating to violence against women in Pakistan are intimately bound up with the legal system, and more specifically with the Hudood Ordinances, which set out different legal statuses for women and men. The other major issue is that of family honour, which is felt to be violated if there is any suspicion that a woman has had sexual intercourse with a man she is not married to. Violated male honour may result in the murder of the offending woman, in some cases, purely on the suspicion of illicit sexual relations.[42]

SENEGAL: In Senegal, there is a law protecting women against all forms of conjugal violence.[43]

VARIOUS LOOPHOLES OF THE ACT

The intention of the Protection of Women from Domestic Violence Act, 2005 is laudable, the Act itself is draconian and very harsh on men. Following are the some of the flaws of the act:

1. The term "domestic violence" defined in section 2(f) of the Act provides that domestic relationship will mean a relationship in which two persons are or have lived together in a shared household. The term shared household by way of common sense means sharing of a household by two or more persons. But this concept has been understood by the legislature in a totally absurd and ambiguous way to even include living singly. Living singly by no stretch of imagination can be understood to be sharing a household.[44]
2. According to the National Family Survey on domestic violence only 25% of the violence is caused by men and out of it a very small number is committed by husbands, while a full 75% of the violence is perpetrated by the women. The finding is not surprising since men tend to put the welfare of women over their own welfare. Indian men unlike Western counterparts look at it as lifelong commitment and that is why this finding is not unsurprising whereas the blood male & female relative treat her as a burden to be passed on and hence they contribute to the violence against women more.[45] And this act adversely effects.
3. The most important flaw in the Act is the inclusion of live-in partners or any sexual partners. This automatically gives legitimacy to live-in relationship and this is unfair for legally wedded wives. Moreover, the act has failed to describe what is "live-in-relationship" in a strict sense? It is creating a situation where the rights of the prostitutes and normal women have been made equal and there is no difference at all.
4. Domestic laws are enacted to save the poor females; but there have been many cases where many cunning unscrupulous women have misused these laws to their advantages. Even women staying outside India, like USA or UK or Dubai or Australia filling the complaints under the Domestic Violence Act just to harass and extort the money from their husbands or their families in India. The Domestic Violence Act has now actually become a powerful tool in the hands of women

to harass men and strip them off all their rights. This Act has actually worsen the domestic problems leading to breakdown in marriages as women will now be encouraged to go to courts after trivial fights or heavy fights happening in the heat of the moment. It discourages women to rectify their mistakes. It not only gives sweeping powers to females but also takes away all the rights of men.

5. Another flaw is regards custody of children. It has upheld the traditional notion of women as children making machines. A husband or mother-in-law who has raised his children could go to Jail merely on account of taking care of children. That there are reports of such happening raises further cause for complaint.[46]
6. Another loophole is arrests happening in domestic violence law for non presence. Civil and marital law does not envision arrests or arrest warrants (the only arrest warrants should be for non compliance of orders not for non presence where in ex parte order may be granted).[47]
7. Section 24 of Hindu Marriage Act, 1955 provides maintenance *pendete lite* to the legitimate relations and similarly, Section 125 of Criminal Procedure, 1973 provides maintenance but not recognizes illegitimate relations. And this act protects cunning women and illegitimate relations. This will create chaos and conflict in the society as what to opt and what not to.
8. As per the definition of respondent in section 2(q) of the Act and as per the interpretation of this section by the court in the case of *Nand Kishore v. State of Rajasthan*[48], it enables the wife or female living in a relationship in the nature of marriage to file a complaint against any relative of the husband or male relative but the most important loophole is that it does not enable any female relative of the husband or the male partner to file a complaint against the wife or the female partner.
9. More than two years have been passed to the coming force of this act but it is contemptible to say that still the appointment of Service Provider and Protection Officer, as provided under the provisions of the act, have not been made. Child Development Protection Officer (CDPO) has been designated this duty and is a single post in each district. Moreover, as per according to the Protection of Women from Domestic Violence Rules, 2006 CDPO is not qualified for the post of Service Provider.
10. No doubt, it is mentioned in the act that the cases will be disposed off within a period of 6 months from the date of first hearing but there is a long delay in the service process as summons are served through ordinary server, and in this way, it takes a long time which is the clear violation of the law itself.

11. It does not provide strict punishment for the guilty and abusive respondents.

CONCLUSION

The various provisions of Constitution, Laws, Acts, Rules, Commissions, Conventions, and Declarations are there and the Protection of Women from Domestic Violence Act, 2005 also has been enacted to prohibit violence against the women and to provide her equal status to men but still there exists the wide gaps and the position of woman is pity. The main reason responsible for this is the difference between the theory and its practicable implementation. So, there is a need that it should be properly implemented and is to be treated and perceived as seriously as any other kind of violence inflicted outside the home. Finally it can be concluded that,

> *"The Woman was made out of a rib out of the side of Adam; not of his feet to be trampled on by him, but one of his side to be equal with him, under his arms to be protected and, near to his heart to be loved."*
>
> Mathew Henry, Exposition of Genesis, 1725.

Notes

1. Gurkirat Kaur, *Women and the Law*, Shree publishers $ distributors, New Delhi, 2005, p.172.
2. Justice Palok Basu, *Law Relating to Protection of Human Rights Under the Indian Constitution and Allied Laws*, Modern Law Publications, Allahabad, 2002, p. 228.
3. Rattan Lal Dhiraj Lal, *Law Lexicon*, Wadhwa Nagpur Publishers, Nagpur.
4. Suresh Kumar Soni (ed.), *Human Rights- Concepts, Issues and Emerging Problems*, Regal Publishers, New Delhi, 2007, p. 52.
5. *The Blackwell Dictionary of Sociology*, Blackwell Publishing, USA, 2005.
6. *Pragati Varghese v. Cyril George Varghese*, A.I.R. 1997 Bom 349.
7. Rhona M. Smith and Christien Van Den Anker (ed.), *The Essentials of Human Rights*, Hodder Arnold, London, 2005, p. 359.
8. Victor De Jouy, Sylla, 1823.
9. Qur'an 81:8-9 Quoted in Rattan Singh and Varinder Singh (ed.), *Socio-Economic Offences in India*, Allahabad Agency, Haryana, 2008, p. 349.
10. *Aziz Mohd. v. Mst. Sayda Begum*, A. I. R. 1981 NOC 55, *Surkhi Ram v. Raj Dulari* 2001 Cr.L.J. 1991 (J $ K).
11. Indira Jaising, *Law of Domestic Violence*, Universal Law Publishing Co. Pvt. Ltd., Delhi, 2001, p. 87.
12. Marjorie Agosin (ed.), *Women, Gender, and Human Rights- A Global Prespective*, Rawat Publications, New Delhi, 2001, p. 87.
13. *Ibid*, p. 88.
14. Section 2(f) of Protection of Women from Domestic Violence Act, 2005.
15. Section 2(s) of Protection of Women from Domestic Violence Act, 2005.

16. Section 2(a) of Protection of Women from Domestic Violence Act, 2005.
17. Section 2(q) of Protection of Women from Domestic Violence Act, 2005.
18. A. I. R. 2008 Raj. 2383 (NOC).
19. Section 3 of Protection of Women from Domestic Violence Act, 2005.
20. *www.expressindia.com* visited on 18th Dec., 2008.
21. *Id.*
22. Section 8 of Protection of Women from Domestic Violence Act, 2005.
23. Section 9 of Protection of Women from Domestic Violence Act, 2005.
24. Section 18 of Protection of Women from Domestic Violence Act, 2005.
25. Section 17 of Protection of Women from Domestic Violence Act, 2005.
26. Section 19 of Protection of Women from Domestic Violence Act, 2005.
27. P. S. Narayana and P. Jagadish Chandra Prasad, *Law Relating to Protection of Human Rights,* Alt Publications, Hyderabad, 2006, p. 286.
28. A. I. R. 2007 SC 1118.
29. Section 10 of Protection of Women from Domestic Violence Act, 2005.
30. Section 20 of Protection of Women from Domestic Violence Act, 2005.
31. Section 21 of Protection of Women from Domestic Violence Act, 2005.
32. Section 22 of Protection of Women from Domestic Violence Act, 2005.
33. Section 23 of Protection of Women from Domestic Violence Act, 2005.
34. A.I.R. 2008 Raj. 1372 (NOC).
35. Section 12 (4), (5) of Protection of Women from Domestic Violence Act, 2005.
36. *www.vakilno.1.com* visited on 18th Dec., 2008.
37. *Id.*
38. *www.feminist.com* visited on 22nd Dec., 2008.
39. *www.bt.com.bn.com* visited on 19th Dec., 2008.
40. *www.bridge.com* visited on 19th Dec., 2008.
41. *Id.*
42. *Id.*
43. *Id.*
44. Nirmal Chopra, The Protection of Women from Domestic Violence Act, 2005-Immorality Legalised, *Criminal Law Journal,* March 2007, p. 54.
45. *www.genderindian.sulekha.com* visited on 22nd Dec., 2008.
46. *www.practicallawyer.ebc-india.com* visited on 22nd Dec., 2008.
47. *Id.*
48. A. I. R. 2008 Raj. 2383 (NOC).

Domestic Violence against Women in India

Santhana Muthu D.* & Arunachalam P.**

INTRODUCTION

Anti-Violence activism for women in India has been riddled with a unique advocacy challenge. Women experiencing violence with the home confront a widespread backlash against Penal Code Section 498A, the only criminal law in India that specifically encompasses domestic violence. The term 'domestic violence' denotes violence occurring within the private circle, generally between individuals who are related through intimacy, blood or law. Analysis of this case reveals that this prohibition against marital cruelty has been drastically undermined by a level of skepticism that not only permeates societal consciousness, but more perilously, has entered judicial-making in these cases (Sharmila Lodhia, 2009). In response to high mortality and morbidity linked with illegal abortion and also in case of girl baby found in the womb, the Indian Medical Termination of Pregnancy (MTP) Act came into force in 1972 for the protection of feminine gender in India (Manisha Gupta *et al.*, 1997).

In 1971, a committee on the status of women was appointed to dissect the position of women. The report of the committee entitled 'Towards Equality' published in 1974 (Sushila Ramasamy, 2005) made a conclusion that women's impact in politics is marginal even though numerically they are the single largest minority. The committee suggested that each political party set a quota for women as a remedial measure and recommended for reserving seats for women in municipal councils and panchayats, and that was done by the 73rd and 74th amendments in 1992. However, at the national level the women reservation bill continues to be in the process of amendment.

* *Research Scholar, Department of Economics, Manonmaniam Sundaranar University, Tirunelveli.*

** *Faculty Member and Head (2004-07) Department of Applied Economics, Cochin University of Science and Technology, Cochin, Kerala State.*

One of the most common forms of violence against women is that done by her husband or by an intimate partner and it is not peculiar to India alone but around the Globe, and the world community of late has accepted its universality and correctly identified it as a violence of human rights, a major health problem and a global epidemic (WTO 2002). Women in India lead a lifetime of ill treatment in various forms such as malnutrition, poor health, lack of education, overwork, dowry related murders. Violence against women in India begins before birth, as sex-selective abortions, female feticides and infanticides, and these continue throughout their lives. Cultural biases and the strong patriarchal social order, with its misplaced notions of masculinity and manhood, find reflections in domestic violence and controlling behaviours of husbands and their wives. Physical abuse of Indian women is reported in various studies such as Mahajan and Madhurima (1995), Jejeebhoy (1998), and Pandey G K *et al* (2009).

According to Rob Stephenson *et al.* (2006), over the past decade, there has been growing recognition of the scope of domestic violence globally and the implications of such violence for the health and well being of women, children and families. They say that evidence from developing countries suggests that anywhere from 10% to 60% of married women of reproductive age report having ever experienced some form of domestic violence, with some of the highest recorded levels coming from South Asia and the domestic violence affects a range of health outcomes, both for the women who experience it and for their children. For women, the consequences associated with domestic violence include physical injury, chronic pain and gas trointestinal symptoms and adverse mental health outcomes. Negative reproductive health outcomes linked to violence include non use of contraception or condoms and unintended pregnancy. For children, they say that an association between domestic violence and low birth weight and prematurely and elevated risks of pre natal and early childhood mortality.

They have further stated that domestic violence may also be associated with gynecologic morbidity. Empirical evidence on this issue, however, comes largely from clinic based studies done in developed country settings; there is a dearth of evidence from population based studies in developing countries and they have found a sample of 3642 couples from northern India (UP State), overall 37% of men have stated that they had committed one or more acts of physical or sexual violence against their wives in the past 12 months, with 12% reporting physical violence only, 17% sexual violence only and 9% both physical and sexual violence. Thirty-four per cent of women reported at least one symptom of gynecologic morbidity compared with women whose husbands reported no violence, those who have experienced both physical and sexual violence and those who had experienced sexual violence only had elevated odds of reporting gynecologic symptoms and Jayaseelan *et al.*, (2007) study which was conducted in rural, urban and urban-slums areas across seven sites in India also expressed the similar view. They found that of 9938 women surveyed, 26% reported experiencing spousal physical violence during the lifetime of their marriage. Adjusted odds ratios calculated using multiple logistic regression analysis suggests that women whose husbands regularly consumed alcohol, reported high physical abuse. The study further says that higher socio economic status and good social support acted as protective buffers against spousal physical violence.

Aparna Mitra and Pooja Singh's (2007) in their study on Kerala State women in India found that high educational attainment has fostered new aspirations and attitudes among women in Kerala and yet society and cultural norms still dictate that women should be subservient to men both at home and in the labour market. Therefore, according to the study, this imbalance often contributes to family violence and suicides in Kerala. This paper predicts that beneath the veil of development lie some disturbing social, cultural and economic issues that may be contributing to high rates of suicide and family violence in Kerala.

BACKGROUND TO DOMESTIC CIVIL LEGISLATION IN INDIA

The Indian government's decision to pass legislation to prevent domestic violence follows from its being a signatory to the UN Convention of Elimination of all forms of Discrimination Against Women (CEDAW) 1989, and its acceptance of the recognition of women's rights as human rights that was included in the Vienna Accord 1994 and the Beijing Women's Conference 1995. Other countries that have similar legislation against domestic violence include the US, Britain, Mauritius, Australia, New Zealand, Malaysia and South Africa.

The Indian Government tabled the Bill in Parliament on 8th March 2002, the International women's Day; but it did not come up for vote because of lack of time during the particular session. In the mean time, various women's movements started a major campaign against many aspects of the proposed law. In response to the strong opposition from these groups, a Parliamentary Standing Committee for the Government's Ministry of Human Resource Development was set up to re-examine the Bill, and its report was put before Parliament in December 2002. It awaits adoption and passage into law at the time of writing (September 2003). Except on two issues, the matter of defining domestic violence and the choice of Magistrate's rather than Civil Courts, the Standing Committee has now accepted the objections made by women's groups and the alternatives and modifications suggested by them. In connection with the above said law, the Indian Government enacted another law called 'the protection of women from domestic violence Act 2005' on 13th September 2005. The Act has given the definition of domestic violence different forms.

For the purpose of the domestic violence Act 2005, omission and commission or conduct of the respondent shall constitute domestic violence in case it-harms or injures or endangers the health, safety, life, limb or well-being, whether mental or physical of the aggrieved person or tends to do so and includes causing physical abuse, sexual abuse, verbal and emotional abuse and economic abuse; or

(a) harasses, harms, injures or endangers the aggrieved person with a view to coerce her or any other person related to her to meet any unlawful demand for any dowry or other property or valuable security; or

(b) has the effect of threatening the aggrieved person or any person related to her by any conduct mentioned in clause (a) or clause (b); or (d) otherwise injures or causes harm, whether physical or mental, to the aggrieved person.

Explanation I-for the purposes of this Section,

(i) 'Physical abuse' means any act or conduct which is of such a nature as to cause bodily pain, harm, or danger to life, limb or health or impair the health or development of the aggrieved person and includes assault, criminal intimidation and criminal force;

(ii) 'Sexual abuse' includes any conduct of a sexual nature that abuses, humiliates, degrades or otherwise violates the dignity of women;

(iii) 'Verbal and emotional abuse' includes- (a) insults, ridicule, humiliation, name calling and insults or ridicule specially with regard to not having a child or a male child; and (b) repeated threats to cause physical pain to any person in whom the aggrieved person is interested.

(iv) 'Economic abuse' includes- (a) deprivation of all or any economic or financial resources to which the aggrieved person is entitled under any law or custom whether payable under an order of a court or otherwise or which the aggrieved person requires out of necessity including, but not limited to household. Necessities for the aggrieved person and her children, if any property jointly or separately owned by the aggrieved person, payment of rental related to the shared household and maintenance; (b) disposal of household effects, any alienation of assets whether movable or immovable, valuable, shares, securities, bonds and the like or other property in which the aggrieved person has an interest, or is entitled to use by virtue of the domestic relationship or which may be reasonably required by the aggrieved person or her children or any other property jointly or separately held by the aggrieved person; and (c) prohibition or restriction to continued access to resources or facilities which the aggrieved person is entitled to use or enjoy by virtue of the domestic relationship including access to the shared household.

DIFFERENT SORTS OF DOMESTIC VIOLENCE WITH DIFFERENT RESEARCH STUDIES IN INDIA

Suneeta Krishnan *et al.,* (2009) have undertaken a study to examine the association between key economic aspects of gender-based power, namely spousal employment status, and physical domestic violence in 2005-06 in Bangalore, India. According to their study, women who were unemployed at one visit and began employment by the next visit has an 80% higher odds of violence, as compared to women who maintained their unemployed status. The study further says that similarly, women whose husbands had stable employment at one visit and newly had difficulty with employment has 1.7 times the odds of violence, as compared to women whose husbands maintained their stable employment. Pradeep Panda and Binda Agarwal (2005) who studied marital violence, human development and women's property status in Kerala, India said that women owning immovable property (land or house) are found to face a significantly lower risk of marital violence than property less women.

Deepthi Varma *et al.*, (2007) assessed pregnant women (no.203) attending as antenatal Clinic in a public hospital in Bangalore, India for presence of Intimate partner violence (IPV)as well as depressive, somatic and Post-Traumatic Stress Disorder (PTSD). The results of the study say that self-reported physical violence in the last year was reported by 14.8 per cent of women, Psychological abuse by 15 per cent, and sexual coercion by 9 per cent. One half of these women reported ongoing abuse during pregnancy. Depression, somatic, and PTSD symptoms were higher in those with a history or sexual coercion, and life satisfaction was poorer in those with any form of violence. The study further says that among those reporting a history of sexual coercion, severity of violence was related to increased psychiatric morbidity and alcohol abuse in the spouse was a predictor of the presence and severity of abuse.

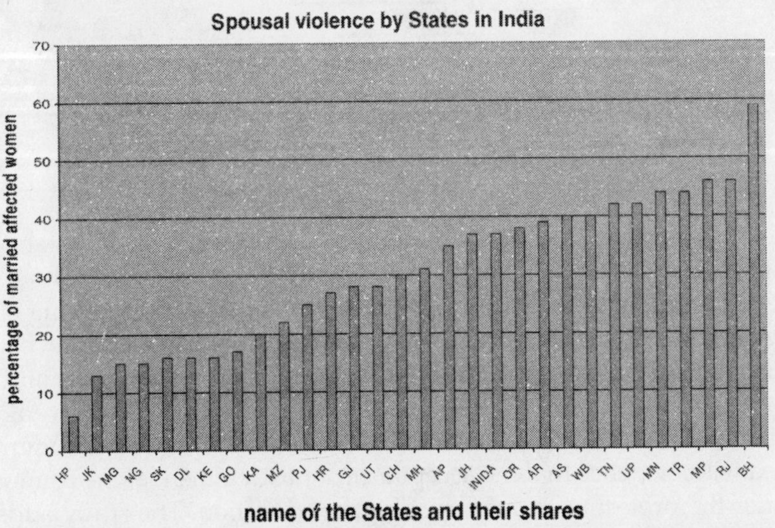

Chart 1

Source: National Family Health Survey Report

The above chart shows the percentage of affected married women by domestic violence in India. According to the figure, Himachel Pradesh State women is least affected by domestic violence and Bihar is the State which is the worst affected by domestic violence against women. Through the chart, we can make conclusion that the States economic development also plays very vital role in reducing domestic violence against women in India.

The Chart 2 shows the factors behind spouse violence in India. According to the Chart, alcohol plays very vital role in the domestic violence against women in India. But still many States in India opening up liquor shops in their territories and it seems they are not taking serious steps to curb domestic violence against women in India.

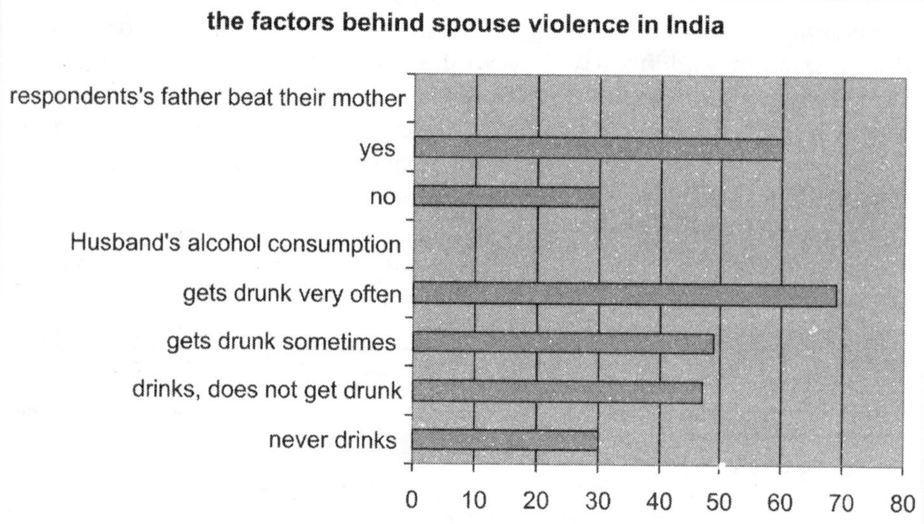

Chart 2

Source: National Family Health Survey

Micheal H Boyle *et al.,* (2009) study also based on IPV in India and their study talked about National Family Health Survey conducted throughout India in 1998-99. According to their study, IPV showed substantial clustering of both the State (10.2%) and community levels (11.5%). At the individual level, there was a strong non-linear association between women's education and IPV, partially accounted for by household living standards. The strength of association between women's education and IPV varied from one community to the next with evidence that the acceptance of mistreatment at the community level mutes the protective influence of higher education. The study adds that women's attitudes towards mistreatment and their standards of living accounted for community level association between women's education and IPV. Suniti Solomon *et al.,* (2009) have examined the prevalence of physical and sexual violence among 1974 married women from 40 low-income communities in Chennai, India. They was found that a 99% and 75% lifetime prevalence of physical abuse and force sex, respectively, whereas 65% of women experienced more than five episodes of physical abuse in the 3 months preceding the study. The study further adds that these domestic violences against women rates exceeds those in prior Indian reports, suggesting women in slums may be at increased risk for HIV and other sexually transmitted infections. Prachi Sanghavi et al., (2009) have studied whole India about fire related deaths in 2001. They have estimated over 163000 fire related deaths in 2001 in India which about 2% of all deaths and about 106000 of these deaths occurred in women, mostly between 15 and 34 years of age. They have identified that the high frequency of fire-related deaths in young women share common causes including Kitchen accidents, Self-immolation, and different form of domestic violence. Corinne H Rocca's *et al.,* (2008) study based on married slum women in Bangalore, India, and it says that nearly 56% participants reported having ever experienced physical domestic violence and about 27% reported violence in past 6 months. Women with love marriage and dowry related problem also reported violence against them and Shin Y Kind et al., (2009) say 7% of pregnant women died due to domestic violence in a rural service units in Vellore, India.

Sharada Srinivasan and Arjun S Bedi (2007) argued through their study based on domestic violence and dowry from South India that larger dowry reduce martial violence by increasing the economic resources of the martial household, enhancing the social status of the groom and his family, and serving as an asset over which the women enjoys relatively more control. The study cautioned that while women with generous dowries may benefit, a continued upward spiral in dowry expectations will exacerbate daughter aversion and may fuel sex selective abortion and female infanticide. Uma A Segal (1999) identified many faces of physical family maltreatment of women-spouse, child, elder, violence against women is not a peculiar case in India but around the world Claudia Garcia-Moreno *et al.,* (2006) and Mary Ellsberg *et al.,* (2008) WHO multi-country studies also revealed about domestic violence against women in different parts of the Globe. Bhatt R V (1998) found that that the use of tobacco, alcohol and narcotic drugs are responsible in aggravating the violence against women and incidence of domestic violence is significantly higher in substance abusers than others. He further adds that it is equally present in countries where the status of women is high, and education level and economic status does not affect the incidence of domestic violence against females. Sesha Kethineni and Murugesan Srinivasan (2009) found that women in Chennai, India who face domestic violence prefer to bring their petitions to women police station for possible solution either through mediation and negotiation or through formal justice process. The authors say that as the family disputes are sensitive, the women police do not immediately intimate legal process through filing of First Information Report (FIR). The following table shows the numbers of different crimes against women are raising but the rate of conviction is decreasing which very dangerous sign for a democracy like India and that will give more confident for the offenders to do crimes against women.

Table 1
Crime against Women in India in 2006 & 2007

Crime Heads	*Cases reported*	*% of total IPC Crimes*	*Rate of crimes*	*Charge sheeting rate*	*Conviction rate*
Kidnapping & adduction	*17414*	*0.9*	*1.6*	*78.1*	*27.6*
of women & girls	20416	1.0	1.8	77.0	25.2
Molestation	*36617*	*1.9*	*3.3*	*96.1*	*30.7*
	38734	1.9	3.4	96.4	29.0
Sexual Harassment	*9966*	*0.5*	*0.9*	*98.2*	*51.8*
	10950	0.6	1.0	97.3	49.9
Cruelty by husband and	*63138*	*3.4*	*5.6*	*94.1*	*21.9*
relatives	75930	3.8	6.7	93.9	20.9
Importation of girls	*67*	*0.0*	*0.0*	*72.0*	*33.3*
	61	0.0	0.0	92.1	11.9
Total crime against women	*164765*	*8.8*	*14.7*	*93.5*	*31.3*
	185312	9.3	16.3	93.2	29.0

Source: National Crime Records Bureau
Note: The Italic numbers are for the year 2006 and others for 2007.

The Table 2 shows the crime head-wise incidents of crime against women during 2002-2006. According to the table, torture and dowry related crimes against women are rising every year and from the data, it is very clear that

Table 2
Crime Head-wise Incidents of Crime against Women during 2002-2006 and Percentage Variation in 2006 over 2005

	Year					
Crime Head	*2002*	*2003*	*2004*	*2005*	*2006*	*% variation in 2006 over 2005*
Rape (Sec. 376 IPC)	16373	15847	18233	18359	19348	5.4
Kidnapping & Abduction (Sec.363 to 373 IPC)	14506	13296	15578	15750	15414	10.6
Torture (Sec. 498A IPC)	49237	50703	58121	58319	63128	8.2
Dowry death (Sec. 302/304 B IPC)	6822	6208	7026	6787	7618	12.2
Molestation (Sec. 354 IPC)	33943	32939	34567	34175	36617	7.1
Sexual Harassment (Sec. 509 IPC)	10155	12325	10001	9984	9966	-0.2
Importation of Girls (Sec. 366-B IPC)	76	46	89	149	67	-55.0
Sati Prevention Act 1987	0	0	0	1	0	-100.0
Immoral Traffic (P) Act 1956	6598	5510	5748	5908	4541	-23.1
Indecent Rep.of women (P) Act, 1986	2508	1043	1378	2917	1562	-46.5
Dowry Prohibition Act 1961	2816	2684	3592	3204	4504	40.6

Source: www.mppolice.gov.in

torture and dowry related crimes are interrelated with each other. Due to unsatisfactory dowry, the bride is being tortured by groom and his family members. In order to eradicate the social evil, the governments (both Central and States) have to come together to enact stringent laws against the law breakers.

DOWRY RELATED VIOLENCE AGAINST WOMEN IN INDIA

Dowry related violence against women most prevalent all over India because in society, there is a custom that is, dowry should be given to a man who is getting married to a woman (but it is prohibited in the Indian Law). Vijayendra Rao's (1997) found that wife abuse is more when dowries are perceived as inadequate and the cause is perceived as legitimate by the community. There is a significant changes have occurred in the practice of dowry in South India. It has become a euphemism for strategies to acquire higher standards of material life, status and security, with negative consequences to women's status, including their survival. This was argument put forth by Sharada Srinivasan (2003. She further stated that the anti-female bias of the practice cannot be tackled from within the dowry trap. Therefore, she suggested that raising the critical consciousness of women about their identity and self-esteem remains a critical component of effective strategies and Jane Rudd (2001) suggested to curb dowry related violence against women through Indian women's movement. Sharmistha Self and Richard Grabowski (2009) have commented that the practice of dowry has rapidly spreading to regions in India where previously it was not extensively practiced and dowry inflation may be occurring and they have said that there are inter caste marriage occurred, net dowry remains unchanged. Sonia Dalmia's (2004) study results indicate that dowries are higher in regions more to the North India and most importantly, contrary to popular belief, their paper found that holding Groom characteristics constant, real dowries have decreased overtime in India.

Linda Stone and Caroline James (1995) have found that that an increasing number of dowry murders have been reported from India and these are cases of married women being murdered, usually burned to death, by husbands or in-laws whose demands for more dowry from bride's family remain unmet. They added that bride-burnings not only reflect women's relative lack of economic power in modern India, but might also reflect a diminishing of the power Indian women traditionally exercised through their family. Manoj Kumar Mohanty *et al.*, (2004) have found that dowry related crimes against women are 30.7% and majority of them were from Hindu religion, majority of them were married, illiterate and drawn from low-socio economic status and rural community.

INTIMATE PARTNER VIOLENCE AGAINST WOMEN

According to Deepthi Varma *et al.*, (2007), the experience of Intimate Parner Violence (IPV) and its mental health consequences are quite prevalent in India which is a culture where gender disparities are normative and pregnancy is a particularly vulnerable period. IPV directed towards women is a serious public health problem. Women's education may give protection against IPV, but uncertainty exists over how it might reduce risk for IPV at the community and individual levels. The IPV against women is not peculiar to India but throughout the world as well. For example, there in Jordan (Cari Jo Clark *et al.*, 2009), in Haiti (Anastasia J Gage 2005), in Spain (Isabel Ruiz-Perez *et al.*, 2006), in Bangladesh (Decker M R *et al.*, 2008), in Sub-Saharan Africa (Olalekan Abdulrahman Uthman *et al.*, 2009), in Pacific Islands (Wanzhen Gao *et al.*, 2008), in Peru (Swee May Cripe *et al.*, 2008), in Canada (Ramona Alaggia *et al.*, 2009), and in Columbia (Christina C Pallitto and Patricia O'Campo 2005).

INTIMATE PARTNER VIOLENCE'S CAUSES AND PREVENTION

Unlike many health problems, there are a few social and demographic characteristics that define risk groups for IPV. Poverty is the exception and increases risk through effects on conflict, women's power and male's identity, and violence is used as a strategy in conflict. Heavy alcohol consumption of male also increases the risk of violence. Women who are more empowered educationally, economically, and socially are the most protected, but below this high level relationship between empowerment and risk of violence is non linear. Violence is often used to resolve a crisis of male identity, at times caused by poverty or an inability to control women. Risk of violence is the greatest in communities where the use of violence in many situations is a socially-accepted norm. Therefore, it is suggested that primary preventive interventions should focus on improving the status of women and reducing norms of violence, poverty and alcohol consumption (Rachel Jewkes, 2002).

CONCLUSION

The problem has to be visualized in a wider context and cannot be viewed in isolation from the status of women in the society. Law alone cannot by itself solve the deep-rooted social problems and one has to approach them in other ways too. What is required is not only a strong legal support network but also opportunities for economic independence, essential education and awareness, alternative accommodation and a change in attitude and mindset of society, judiciary, legislative, executive, men and the most important women herself. Restructuring society in terms of power and role of relationship while emphasizing the egalitarian values is the need of the day. To overcome from violence against women in India it is suggested to ensure a proportional representation of women in the national political system.

References

Anastasia J. Gage (2008), "Women's Experience of Intimate Partner Violence in Haiti", *Social Science & Medicine*, Vol. 61, Issue 2, July, pp. 343-364.

Aparna Mitra and Pooja Singh (2007), "Human Capital Attainment and Gender Empowerment: The Kerala Paradox", *Social Science Quarterly*, Vol. 88, No. 5, December, pp. 1227-1242.

Bhatt R. V. (1998), "Domestic Violence and Substance Abuse", *International Journal of Gynecology & Obstetrics*, Vol. 63, Supplement 1, December, pp. S25-S21.

Cari Jo Clark *et al.*, (2009), "The Role of Extended Family in Women's Risk of Intimate Partner Violence in Jordan", *Social Science & Medicine*, Available online 16 October.

Chritina C. Pallitto and Patricia O'Campo (2005), "Community Level Effects of Gender Inequality on Intimate Partner Violence and Unintended Pregnancy in Columbia: Testing the Feminist Perspective", *Social Science & Medicine*, Vol. 60, Issue 10, May, pp. 2205-2216.

Claudia Garcia-Moreno, Henrica AFM Gansen, Mary Ellsberg, Lori Heise, Charlotte H Watts and on Behalf of the WHO Multi-country Study on Women's Health and Domestic Violence against Women Study Team (2006), "Prevalence of Intimate Partner Violence: Findings from the WHO Multi-country Study on Women's Health and Domestic Violence", *The Lancet*, Vol. 368, Issue 9543, October, pp. 1260-1269.

Corinne H. Rocca, Sujit Rathod, Tina Falle, Rohini P. Pande and Suneetha Krishnan (2009), "Challenging Assumptions about Women's Empowerment: Social and Economic Resources and Domestic Violence among Young Married Women in Urban South India", *International Journal of Epidemiology*, Vol. 38, No. 2, April, pp. 577-585.

Decker M R *et al.*, (2008), "Intimate Partner Violence and Sexually Transmitted Disease Symptoms in a National Sample of Married Bangladeshi Women", *International Journal of Gynecology & Obstetrics*, Vol. 100, Issue 1, January, pp. 18.23.

Deepthi Varma, Prabha S. Chandra, Tinku Thomas and Micheal P. Carey (2007), "Intimate Partner Violence and Sexual Coercion among Pregnant Women in India: Relationship with Depression and Post-traumatic Stress Disorder", *Journal of Affective Disorders*, Vol. 102, Issue 1-3, September, pp. 227-235.

Isabel Ruiz-Perez *et al.*, (2006), "Socio Demographic Associations of Physical, Emotional, and Sexual Intimate Partner Violence in Spanish Women", *Annals of Epidemiology*, Vol. 16, Issue 5, pp. 357-363.

Jane Rudd (1001), "Dowry-murder: An Example of Violence against Women", *Women's Studies International Forum*, Vol. 24, Issue 5, September-October, pp. 513-522.

Jejeebhoy S. J. (1998), "Association between Wife Beating and Foetal and Infant Death: Impressions from a Survey in Rural India", *Studies in Family Planning*, 29, pp. 300-308.

Jeyaseelan *et al.*, (2007), "Physical Spousal Violence against Women in India: Some Risk Factors", *Journal of Biosocial Science*, Vol. 39, pp. 657-670.

Lauren L. Tichy, Judith V. Becker and Melissa M. Sisco (2009), "The Downside of Patriarchal Benevolence in Addressing Domestic Violence and Socio-Economic Considerations for Women of Tamil Nadu, India", *Journal of Family Violence*, Vol. 24, No. 8, November, pp. 547-558.

Linda Stone and Caroline James (1995), "Dowry, Bride-burning, and Female Power in India", *Women's Studies International Forum*, Vol. 18, Issue 2, March-April, pp. 125-134.

Madhu Mehra (1998), "Exploring the Boundaries of Law, Gender and Social Reform", *Feminist Legal Studies*, Vol. VI, No. 1, pp. 59.85.

Mahajan A. and O. Madhurima (1995), "Family Violence and Abuse in India, New Delhi, India", Deep and Deep Publications, New Delhi.

Manisha Gupte, Sunita Bandewar and Hemlata Pisal (1997), "Abortion Needs of Women in India" A Case Study of Rural Maharastra", *Reproductive Health Matters*, Vol. 5, Issue 9, pp. 77-86.

Manoj Kumar Mohanty, Manoj Kumar Panigrahi, Sachidananda Mohanty and Sirmanta Kumar Das (2004), "Victimiologic Study of Female Homicide", *Legal Medicine*, Vol. 6, Issue 3, July, pp. 151-156.

Mary Ellsberg, Henrica AFM Jansen, Lori Heise, Charlotte H. Watts, Claudia Garcia-Moreno and on behalf of Who multi-country study on women's health and domestic violence against women study team (2008), "Intimate partner violence and women's physical and mental health in the WHO multi-country study on women's health and domestic violence: An observational study", *The Lancet*, Vol.371, Issue 9619, April, pp.1165-1172.

Michael H. Boyle, Katholiki Georgiades, John Cullen and Yuonne Racine (2009), "Community Influences on intimate partner violence in India: Women's education, attitudes towards mistreatment and standards of living", *Social Science & Medicine*, Vol. 69, Issue 5, September, pp. 691-697.

National Family Health Survey 2005-06 Report.

Olalekan Abdulrahman Uthman, Tahereh Moradi and Stephen Lawoko (2009), "The independent contribution of individual, neighbourhood, and country-level socio-economic position on attitudes towards intimate partner violence against women in Sub-Saharan Africa: A Multi level model of direct and moderating effects", *Social Science & Medicine*, Vol. 68, Issue 10, May, pp. 1801-1809.

Pandey G K, Debashis Dutt and Bratati Banerjee (2009), "Partner and Relationship Factors in Domestic Violence: Perspectives of Women from a Slum in Calcutta, India", *Journal of Interpersonal Violence*, Vol. 24, No. 7, July, pp. 1175-1191.

Piyush Jain (2006), "Women in India from Brith to Marriage: Oppression and Domestic Violence", *Oxford Journal of Anthropology*, January.

Prachi Sanghavi, Kavi Bhalla and Veena Das (2009), "Fire-related Deaths in India in 2001: A Retrospective Analysis of Data", *Lancet*, Vol. 373, No. 9671, April, pp. 1282-1288.

Pradeep Panda and Binda Aggarwal (2005), "Marital Violence, Human Development and Women's Property Status in India", *World Development*, Vol. 33, Issue 5, May, pp. 823-850.

Rachel Jewkes (2002), "Intimate Partner Violence: Causes and Prevention", *The Lancet*, Vol. 359, Issue 9315, April, pp. 1423-1229.

Rajeswari Sundar Rajan (2004), "Rethinking Law and Violence: The Domestic Violence (Prevention) Bill in India, 2002", *Gender & History*, Vol. 16, No .3, November, pp. 769-793.

Ramona Alaggia, Cheryl Regehr and Giselle Rish Chynski (2009), "Intimate Partner Violence and Immigration Laws in Canada: How far have we come?", *International Journal of Law and Psychiatry*, Vol. 32, Issue 6, Nov.-Dec., pp. 335-341.

Rob Stephenson, Michael A Koenig and Saifuddin Ahmed (2006), "Domestic Violence and Symptoms of Gynecologic Morbidity among Women in North India", *International Family Planning Perspectives*, Vol. 32, No. 4, pp. 201-208.

Sesha Kethineni and Murugesan Srinivasan (2009), "Police Handling of Domestic Violence Cases in Tamil Nadu, India", *Journal of Contemporary Criminal Justice*, Vol. 25, No. 2, May, pp. 202-213.

Sharada Srinivasan (2005), "Daughter or Dowries? The Changing Nature of Dowry Practices in South India", *World Development*, Vol. 33, Issue 4, April, pp. 593-615.

Sharada Srinivasan and Arjun S Bedi (2007), "Domestic Violence and Dowry: Evidence from a South Indian Village", *World Development*, Vol. 35, Issue 5, May, pp. 857-880.

Sharma B. R. (2005), "Social Etiology of Violence against Women in India", *The Social Science Journal*, Vol. 42, Issue 3, pp. 375-389.

Sharmila Lodhia (2009), "Legal Frankenstins and Monstrous Women:*Judical Narratives of the "family in Crisis""*, *Meridians Feminism, Race, Transnationalism*, Vol. 9, No. 2, pp. 102-129.

Sharmistha Self and Richard Grabowski (2009), "Modernization, Inter-caste Marriage, and Dowry: An Analytical Perspective", *Journal of Asian Economics*, Vol. 20, Issue 1, January, pp. 69-76.

Shin Y. Kim, Roger Rochat, Abel Rajaratnam and Ann Digiroiamo (2009), "Evaluating Completeness of Maternal Mortality Rporting in a Rural Health and Social Affairs Unit in Vellore, India, 2004", *Journal of Biosocial Science*, Vol. 41, No. 2, March.

Sonia Dalmia (2004), "A Hedonic Analysis of Marriage Transactions in India: Estimating Determinants of Dowries and Demand for Groom Characteristics in Marriage", *Research in Economics*, Vol. 58, Issue 3, September, pp. 235-255.

Suneetha Krishnan, Corinne H. Rocca, Alan E Hubbard, Kalyani Subbiah, Jeffrey Edmeades and Nancy S. Padian (2009), "Do changes in spousal employment status lead to domestic violence? Insights from a prospective study in Bangalore, India", *Social Science & Medicine*, Available online 14 October.

Suniti Solomon *et al.*, (2009), "Domestic Violence and Forced Sex among the Urban Poor in South India: Implications for HIV Prevetion", *Violence Against Women*, Vol. 15, No. 7, July, pp. 753-773.

Sushila Ramaswamy (2005), "India's Crisis of Governance: The Women's Perspective", *Policy and Society*, Vol. 24, Issue 3, pp. 122-141.

Swee may Cripe *et al.*, (2008), "Association of Intimate Partner Physical and Sexual Violence with Unintended Pregnancy among Pregnant Women in Peru", International Journal of Model of Direct and Moderating Effects", *Social Science & Gynecology & Obstetrics*, Vol. 100, Issue 2, pp. 124-108.

The Protection of Women from Domestic Violence Act, 2005.

Uma A. Segal (1999), "Family Violence: A Focus on India", *Aggression and Violent Behaviour*, Vol. 4, Issue 2, Summer, pp. 213-231.

Viayendra Rao (1997), "Wife-beating in Rural South India: A Quantitative and Econometric Analysis", *Social Science & Medicine*, Vol. 44, Issue 8, April, pp. 1169-1180.

Wanzhen Gao *et al.*, (2008), "Intimate Partner Violence and Unplanned Pregnancy in the Pacific Islands Families Study", *International Journal of Gynecology & Obstetrics*, Vol. 100, Issue 2, February, pp. 109-115.

World Health Organisation (2002), "World Report on Violence and Health", Geneva, Switzerland.

Elder Abuse and Factors

V. S. Ganesamurthy*

INTRODUCTION

World Elders day is celebrated every year on 1st October. But the elders face many problems and in some cases they are abused. Older persons are generally neglected and ignored. The elderly need true love and affection from the younger generation.

Every human being passes through various stages in his life time, birth, infancy, childhood, adolescence, adulthood and old age this biological transition trough different stages has cultural and human overtones.

In Indian society, elderly people are regarded as symbol of the divine and given utmost respect. They are considered as the repositories of wisdom, carriers of traditions and transmitters of experience and ideas of group living. The aged have a definite place in society.

What is Ageing?

Ageing has been viewed different by different persons. To industrialist, it can mean power and wealth, where as to a middle class employee, it amount to forced retirement, for the poor it is a state of dependence. To most ageing implies psychological and psycho-social changes reflected in general physical weakness, decline in sense perception and mental activity and lessening social activities and interest[1] (Dak and Sharma 1987, p. 43).

EFFECT OF OLD AGE

The old age covering the later part of life of an individual, when physical deterioration beings to appear, is generally marked by a shift in an individual position from active social participation to significant decline in role

* *Resear and Head, Department of Economics, Sri Vasavi College Erode-638316*

performance and from economic self-sufficiency to economic dependence. The role deflect and consequent lowering of morale is primarily a problem of adjustment arising out of with drawl from work, poor health and low socio-economic status. Old age is the period when the individual enjoys the fruits of his labour organising leisure time activities. The old have all the time in the world to enjoy life and look back on life. They have the prestige that comes from past achievements solony they have supported their families and now they expect loyalty and gratitude from them.

ECONOMIC CONTRIBUTIONS OF THE AGED

Senior citizens make many contributions that are not measured in economic terms such as care of family members, productive subsistence work, household maintenance and voluntary activities in the community.

WHY CARE IS NEEDED?

Older persons are generally neglected, ignored and in some cases abused. The abuse is more psychological than verbal. The elderly need true love and affection from the younger generation. Ageing is a time of multiple illness and general disability. Along with changes in biological composition life style factors are also important for disorders and diseases in old age.

Growth Rate of Population and Elderly Population in India

Year	*Growth Rate of Population*	*Growth rate of elderly persons*	*Population in billions*
1991	1.99	1.77	0.843
2001	1.50	1.57	1.027
2011*	1.02	2.10	1.19
2021*	0.70	2.95	1.32
2031*	0.40	3.04	1.41
2041*	0.20	3.87	1.47
2051*	-	4.33	1.50

Source: Census Report of India[2]   * Estimated

From the above table, it is cleared that the estimated growth rate of elderly persons is more than that of the growth rate of population.

FACTORS FOR ABUSE OF ELDERS

(1) Migration of younger generation
(2) Dependency
(3) Multiple illness
(4) Social losses with age
(5) Aged persons are increasingly isolated and left out.

(6) Aged persons are considered useless due to technological advancement and its accompanying social change.

(7) Economic problems[3]

(8) Lack of security especially women if they are alone.[4]

(9) Left out by family members.

(10) Human rights violation.

The growing cultural insensitivity to old people contrasts starkly with idolization of youth. Old people should be valued for three wisdom, experience and contribution to society. But in effect they are regarded as a burden to families and the state. The half Jocular lament "The old man wont die and vacate the cot" reduces old people to disposable commodities. No decent society can be insensitive to the moans and cries of pains of the aging population.[5]

CONCLUSION

The elderly should be considered as a valuable human resource and their rich experience and residual capacities should be put to optimum use for the benefit of national development.

Notes and References

1. Dak and Sharma (1987), Ageing in India, Delhi, Ajanta Publishing, p. 43.
2. Census Report of India.
3. Anoop Kumar Bhartiya, "The Aged in India: Policies and Programmes", *Social Welfare,* Oct. 2008, pp. 5-7.
4. *The Hindu* April 15, 2009, Weekly Edition, 2, pp. 1 and 4.
5. World Elders Day, G. David Milton Marthancode, *Indian Express*, Dt. Oct. 2, 2009.

Violence against Women with Special Reference to Dowry Deaths in India

D. PULLA RAO*

INTRODUCTION

Discrimination and exploitation on the basis of gender constitutes a serious issue which effectively means that half the human race is unable to realize its potential and condemned to sub-optional standards of existence. This problem has received worldwide attention and several efforts have been made to bridge the seemingly ever-widening gap. Yet, even after years of efforts to integrate women into the mainstream development process, the effectivity of the same remains to be questioned owing to a multitude of factors which aid the continued marginalization of women. Women's equal access to education, health, employment and political space still remain distant goals in almost all the countries of the world. One of the most serious impediments to women's development is the phenomenon of continuing and increasing violence against them. Needless to say, this constitutes a serious violation of woman's human rights. Gender violence manifests itself in various forms – female foeticide and infanticide, sexual abuse, incest, molestation, sexual harassment at work and on the streets, marital rape, domestic violence in the form of wife assault and women battering. Of all the forms of violence that women face, domestic violence remains the least reported and largely suppressed.

Violence against women is socially a very sensitive issue and more so in our country where we have a special place for 'Family Honour'. Any act which affects the family honour is not tolerated and very strongly put down. Therefore the acts of violence are seldom talked-out of the family and its close confines.

Violence against women is widespread and viewed as one of the cruelest social mechanisms to suppress women. Unequal power relations have led to

* *Department of Economics, Andhra University Visakhapatnam, A.P.*

discrimination against women. Violence on women manifests even before birth and early life, married life as domestic violence, rape, murder, dowry death etc.

The basic reason for violence against women is their inferior status educationally, economically, politically, and socially-in a male dominated society. Other factors responsible for increasing criminalization of society, media images inadequate means to address the cause and consequences of violence's; poor enforcement of legal provisions, unabashed consumerism and erosion of family values have all added to it. Over the past decade, there has been growing awareness of this phenomenon and its long-term impact on women empowerment. The media reports extensively on dowry deaths, rape, molestation, incest, assault etc. and give out information that was virtually unavailable till a few years ago.

CATEGORIES OF VIOLENCE AGAINST WOMAN IN INDIA

Though woman's movement has had a long history of raising various concerns, violence was not the central issue till late seventies. Around late seventies the issues like dowry, wife beating were in the forefront and through them women's concerns were expressed. Initially the measure like legal aid centers and counseling services were taken by the Government and Non-Governmental Organisations. That was the starting point. The issue of violence against woman started coming in to the forefront from early eighties onwards. The issue was widely discussed and advocated due to continuous efforts of woman's organizations and activists. Very broadly, if we want to assess the situation of today, we can categorize violence against women in the following manner:

Violence within family

- Wife beating and battering
- Dowry deaths
- Sexual abuse of female children
- Incest at all stages of a woman's life
- Unwanted pregnancy
- Female foeticide and infanticide
- Alcoholism

- Impact of patriarchal values
- Domination and control within family
- Cultural reasons

Violence within community or society at large

- Sexual Harassment, molestation and intimidation at work
- Rape
- Kidnapping and abduction
- Sexual abuse
- Stripping and shaming of women
- Trafficking
- Forced prostitution
- Caste and communal violence

- Women's rights over their bodies denied
- Feminization of poverty
- commercial Interests of Sex work industry

Violence in difficult circumstances like Wars and Riots

- Rape
- Sexual harassment and abuse

- Occupation by opponent's military
- War crimes

INCIDENCE OF OFFENCES AGAINST WOMEN BY CATEGORY

The data in Table 1 represents incidence of crimes committed against women during1996-2004. Torture (cruelty by husband and relatives) occupies the first place and accounts for 37.66 per cent of crimes followed by molestation (22.40%). Both these crimes account for 55 to 60 per cent during 1996 to 2004. Rape, kidnapping and abduction cases account for 22 to 26 per cent while sexual harassment, dowry death and others account for the rest.

Of the nine categories of violence, crimes such as torture, rape, kidnapping & abduction, dowry death and others have increased in 2004 over 2003. Sexual harassment has decreased from 8.77 per cent in 2003 to 6.48 per cent in 2004 due to the intervention of government and follow up action taken to fulfill the directions of Hon'ble Supreme Court.

Andhra Pradesh (with 7.3% of population) has accounted for 12.3 per cent of total incidents of crime (18921 cases) in 2004. Uttar Pradesh (with 16.4% population), has accounted for 10.0 per cent of crime against women (115485 cases) in 2004. Six states viz., Andhra Pradesh (12.3%) Uttar Pradesh (9.9%), Rajasthan (8.5%), Maharashtra (7.9%), and West Bengal (7.2 %) contribute 56 per cent of total crimes in 2004.

Table 1

Category-wise Incidence of Crime in India: 1996-2004

Types of crimes	*1996*	*1997*	*1998*	*1999*	*2000*	*2001*	*2002*	*2003*	*2004*	*Growth Rate (1996-2004) %*
Torture	35246	36592	41376	43823	45778	49170	49237	50703	58121	64.9
	(30.46)	(30.18)	(31.47)	(32.28)	(32.38)	(34.19)	(34.42)	(36.06)	(37.66)	
Molestation	28939	30764	30959	32311	32940	34124	33943	32939	34567	19.4
	(25.01)	(25.37)	(23.55)	(23.80)	(23.30)	(23.73)	(23.73)	(23.43)	(22.40)	
Rape	14846	15330	15151	15468	16496	16075	16373	15847	18233	22.8
	(12.83)	(12.64)	(11.52)	(11.39)	(11.67)	(11.18)	(11.45)	(11.27)	(11.81)	
Kidnapping &	14877	15617	16351	15962	15023	14645	14506	13296	15578	4.7
Abduction	(12.85)	(12.88)	(12.44)	(11.76)	(10.63)	(10.19)	(10.14)	(9.46)	(10.09)	
Sexual	5671	5796	8054	8858	11024	9746	10.55	12325	10001	76.3
Harassment	(4.90)	(4.78)	(6.13)	(6.52)	(7.80)	(6.78)	(7.10)	(8.77)	(6.48)	
Dowry	5513	6006	6975	6699	6995	6851	6822	6208	7026	27.4
Death	(4.76)	(4.95)	(5.31)	(4.93)	(4.95)	(4.76)	(4.77)	(4.41)	(4.55)	
Immoral	7706	8323	8695	9363	9515	8796	6598	5510	5748	-25.4
Traffic Act	(6.66)	(6.86)	(6.61)	(6.90)	(6073)	(6.12)	(4.61)	(3.92)	(3.72)	
Dowry	2647	2685	3578	3064	2876	3222	2816	2684	3592	35.7
Prohibition Act	(2.29)	(2.22)	(2.72)	(2.26)	(2.03)	(2.24)	(1.97)	(1.91)	(2.33)	
Other Acts	278	151	336	223	726	1166	2584	1089	1467	427.7
	(0.24)	(0.12)	(0.25)	(0.16)	(0.51)	(0.81)	(1.86)	(0.77)	(0.95)	
Total	115723	121264	131475	135771	141373	143795	143034	140601	154333	33.4
	(100)	(100)	(100)	(100)	(100)	(100)	(100)	(100)	(100)	

Source: GOI, Crime in India, 2001, National Crime Records Bureau, 2003 and 2005.

DOWRY

Dowry has been referred to as a social cancer, a cruel custom and an insult to the dignity of women. The dowry problem which aroused as one of the biggest problem to the women community is expanding from the Indian historical traditional context to the today's technological context. The women dowry deaths problem is not simply social exclusion or re-exclusion; it is permanent exclusion from enjoying the Right to Life. It has been crystallised in our society and, despite legislation, cases of dowry harassment and dowry deaths are increasing every year. There are horrific reports of fathers selling kidneys to cover dowry payments, or collective suicides in families with multiple daughters. Surprisingly dowry has spread to all most all communities in India, most of them were traditionally non-dowry taking communities. Although the dowry was legally prohibited in India in 1961, it continues to be highly institutionalized. The practice of dowry abuse is rising in India. The most severe is the "bride burning", the burning of women whose dowries were not considered sufficient by their husband or in-laws. Most of these incidents are reported as accidental burns in the kitchen or are disguised as suicide. It is evident that there exist deep rooted prejudices against women in India. Though prohibited by law in 1961, the extraction of dowry from the bride's family prior to marriage still occurs. When the dowry amount is not considered sufficient or is not forthcoming, the bride is often harassed, abused and burnt down.

DEFINITION OF DOWRY

Dowry or Dahej is the payment in cash or/and kind by the bride's family to the bridegroom's family along with the giving away of the bride (called kanyadaan) in Indian marriage. Kanyadanam is an important part of Hindu marital rites. Kanya means daughter, and dana means gift.

Dowry originated in upper caste families as the wedding gift to the bride from her family. The dowry was later given to help with marriage expenses and became a form of insurance in the case that her in-laws mistreated her.

HISTORICAL BACKGROUND OF DOWRY

The custom of kanyadaan (giving the daughter in marriage) followed by varadakshina (gift to the bridegroom at time of marriage) may have given rise to dowry. It is in the Rig Veda that one comes across the concept of kanyadaan. It was a custom in ancient times to give dakshina (obligatory gifts) after any type of daan (voluntary gifts), hence the tradition of varadakshina following kanyadaan. It is said that Rishi Karav gave a number of gifts to his daughter, Shakuntala, when she married King Dushyant. It can be surmised that, since child marriages was the norm in ancient India, the parents may have given numerous gifts to the girl child as she left her maternal home. However, dowry, as it now exits, involves the extraction of cash and material goods from the bride's parents by the groom and his family.

This social malady has spread through the spectrum of society crossing religious and economic boundaries. Moreover, dowry demands are made not only prior to the wedding, but also for years thereafter, for example, at the time of festivals and the birth of children. Demands for dowry have been camouflaged after the passing of the Dowry Prohibition Act, 1961, and its amendment in 1984. In few cases, demands are made hours before the wedding and there have been instances when the bride's family has cancelled the wedding.

DEFINITION OF DOWRY DEATH

A dowry death is defined as the unnatural death of a woman caused by burns or bodily injury occurring within the first seven years of marriage, if it can be shown that the woman was subjected to cruelty by her husband or her husband's relatives shortly before death in connection with a demand for dowry.

STATUS OF DOWRY DEATHS IN INDIA BY STATES/UTS

Most of the young women in India had lost their lives on the pyre of their husbands in the name of 'sati'. The modern 'dowry deaths' replaced ancient sati pyre. Dowry deaths are the deaths caused young women, where the women is murdered or forced to commit suicide by continuous harassment for more dowry by her husband and in-laws. Dowry deaths are reported in various other south Asian countries also. The practice of women giving a 'dowry' or gift to a man at marriage is said to have had its origins in the system of streedhan (women's share of parental wealth given to her at the time of her marriage). Dowry death is considered as one of the many categories of violence against women. There were about 5,513 dowry death cases registered in India in the year 1996. It increased 6,787 by 2005. The data are drawn from statistics published by the National Crime Bureau of the government of India, which reports about 6,000 dowry deaths from many parts of India every year. But, the reality is worst than what is showed in records some might be after looking at the statistics under impression that there might not be any dowry prohibition act to protect women from the involuntary dowry burnt deaths. Table 2 shows that Andhra Pradesh sands as the top with 13.4 per cent in the case of violence against women occurred in 2005. The highest dowry deaths were recorded in Uttar Pradesh (23%) followed by Bihar (14.9%), Madhya Pradesh (10.9%) and Andhra Pradesh (6.5%). All these statistics are just official records, registered in the government offices, but in reality dowry deaths are much higher than reported.

INVOLVEMENT OF FAMILIES IN DOWRY RELATED VIOLENCE

Dowry harassment and death are psycho-socio-legal issues. There is, therefore, an interplay of many systems in handling the cases of dowry-related violence. The following is a brief description of the roles played by each system.

Table 2
Incidents of Crime and Dowry Deaths Committed against Women in India: 2005

State	*Incidents*	*Percentage Contribution to all India total*	*Rank*	*No. of Dowry Deaths*	*Percentage Contribution to all India total*
Andhra Pradesh	20819	13.4	1	443	6.5
Arunachal Pradesh	150	0.1	24	0	0.0
Assam	6027	3.9	12	99	1.5
Bihar	6019	3.9	13	1014	14.9
Chhattisgarh	3599	2.3	16	100	1.5
Goa	121	0.1	28	2	0.0
Gujarat	6343	4.1	09	48	0.7
Haryana	4161	2.7	15	212	3.1
Himachal Pradesh	793	0.5	21	2	0.0
Jammu & Kashmir	2144	1.4	18	5	0.1
Jharkhand	2544	1.6	17	257	3.8
Karnataka	6057	3.9	11	261	3.8
Kerala	6762	4.3	8	21	0.3
Madhya Pradesh	14529	9.3	3	739	10.9
Maharashtra	13370	8.6	4	341	5.0
Manipur	140	0.1	25	0	0.0
Meghalaya	131	0.1	26	1	0.0
Mizoram	95	0.1	29	4	0.1
Nagaland	37	0.0	31	0	0.0
Orissa	6249	4.0	10	334	4.9
Punjab	1969	1.3	19	99	1.5
Rajasthan	11657	7.5	6	361	5.3
Sikkim	62	0.0	30	0	0.0
Tamil Nadu	8648	5.6	7	215	3.2
Tripura	840	0.5	20	34	0.5
Uttar Pradesh	14875	9.6	2	1564	23.0
Uttaranchal	786	0.5	22	63	0.9
West Bengal	11887	7.6	5	446	6.6
A&N Islands	22	0.0	33	0	0.0
Chandigarh	205	0.1	23	3	0.0
D&N Haveli	24	0.0	32	0	0.0
Daman & Diu	10	0.0	34	1	0.0
Delhi	4351	2.8	14	114	1.7
Lakshadweep	0	0.0	-	0	0.0
Pondicherry	127	0.1	27	4	0.1
Total	155553	100.0		6787	100.0

Source: National Crime Reports Bureau.

THE BRIDE'S PARENTAL FAMILY

It is well-known that in most Indian families the birth of a daughter is not a happy event. A daughter symbolises the sword of Damocles in terms of her marriage, dowry and endless expenses thereafter. Our proverbs amply illustrate the concept of a daughter being a burden. With such a degrading attitude towards the daughter; it is no wonder that parents are eager to marry her off at the earliest opportunity. Child marriages are still prevalent in Bihar, Rajasthan, Madhya Pradesh and Uttar Pradesh. It is as if the bride's parents shift this 'burden' onto the groom and in order to make this burden as light as possible, give a sumptuous dowry. Therefore, parents begin to save money for their daughter's wedding and dowry soon after her birth. One can well imagine the plight of the low and lower middle class and those with more than one daughter.

The girl's parents, thus, are also responsible for the perpetuation of violence related to dowry because:

- They accept this custom by their tacit approval.
- Most of them keep giving in to demands long after the marriage. They think that no sacrifice is too great for their daughter's happiness.
- They are reluctant to lodge a police complaint as they are concerned about the family's prestige. They discourage their daughter, too, from lodging a complaint.
- Generally, parents condition their daughters to be docile. They are told to bear all hardships uncomplainingly.
- Even after their daughter's death, parents feel it is useless to lodge a complaint as the culprit will never be booked. They also feel that since nothing will bring back their dead daughter, it is point less to get into the web of police, lawyers and the judiciary. However, there have been exceptions.
- When the girl finds the harassment unbearable, she returns to her maternal home. But most parents do not encourage their married daughters to stay with them for long periods. Some communities believe that it is a sin to keep a married daughter at home.
- In order to avoid giving an equal share in the self-acquired property to their daughters according to the amended Hindu Succession Act, parents make a will leaving little or nothing to their daughters.

THE GROOM'S FAMILY

The birth of a boy is an occasion for rejoicing. The woman who gives birth to a son gets special favours from her husband and in-laws in some communities. Generally, boys are socially conditioned to feel superior. There is covert or overt discrimination by the parents against their daughters. As the son grows up, dowry expectations are expressed by his parents subtly or openly. A statement like ' We are not buying a washing machine yet, because it will came as part of our son's dowry' convince the young man that dowry is his birthright.

The groom and his family perpetuate the problem because they:

- insist that all expenses for the wedding be borne by the bride's family;

- also decide the menu for the wedding, the decorations and other such formalities;
- demand gifts for themselves and their relatives;
- demand dowry in cash or in kind; and
- initiate the harassment of the bride and continue to do so until she leaves her marital home or is murdered by them, paving the way for a second marriage for the groom and, consequently, to start another dowry ritual.

ANTI DOWRY MOVEMENT IN INDIA

The most severe is the "bride burning", the burning of women whose dowries were not considered sufficient by their husband or in-laws. Most of these incidents are reported as accidental burns in the kitchen or are disguised as suicide. Official records of these incidents are low because they are often reported as accidents or suicides by the family.

Beginning of the anti-dowry movement was in the 1970s and 1980s. The movement appeared to lose steam in the 1990s as women's organisations dealt with a spate of other issues, but problems related to dowry continued to multiply. The women's movement in India is a rich and vibrant movement which has taken different forms in different parts of the country. The Dowry Prohibition (Amendment) Act (1984, 1986) makes the giving and taking of dowry "as a condition of marriage" punishable by law, while excluding "voluntary gifts"- a combination of provisions which makes for toothless sanctions.

The following are some of the movements done by women in India

All India Democratic Women's Association (AIDWA)

It is Tripura state committee of "All India Democratic Women's Association (AIDWA)" Organized a state level convention on dowry system and atrocities against women at Rabindra Bhavan at Agartala. At first the AIDWA state secretary Rama Das expressed deep concern on the rise in atrocities on women in the recent time despite a vigorous campaign by AIDWA committees and active role of the governments. State women's Commission chairperson Champa Dasgupta commended the AIDWA for playing a great role in the state. The AIDWA will hold a series of district and local level conventions against the dowry system, killing of brides and torture against women.

The All India Women's Congress (AIWC)

The AIWC was the first all India women's organization. Its charter explicitly identified the organization with the mainstream struggle for national freedom. Both bourgeois liberals and the Left joined together in the AIWC, and its formation coincided with Mahatma Gandhi's calls in the 1920s to popularize the freedom movement, to sunder the struggle from its upper caste, elite moorings. Thus the AIWC and those associated with it not only saw their role as fighting for the status and rights of women but unambiguously located this task within the agenda of the freedom struggle as a whole. This was the real strength that the women's movement acquired at its birth. It has remained a cherished tradition within the movement, a tradition that still lives and informs the movement through its ups and downs.

Nari Atma Raksha Samity (NARS)

The NARS movement rapidly grew and developed structured links with the organized Left. Members of NARS supported and participated in the historic Tebhaga struggle. Elsewhere in the country, women with Left political leanings were involved in working class and revolutionary peasant struggles, such as the struggle in Telengana proved a very influential learning experience for the Left, illustrating how women could fight.

Anti-Arrack

Anti-arrack movement in Andhra Pradesh grew out the inspiration gained by women in adult literacy classes. In 1992, women of Dubagunta village in Nellore, one of the poor and drought prone districts of Southern Andhra Pradesh, organized and agitated to force the closure of the arrack (liquor) shop in the village. News papers published this story, and women all over the state marched to arrack shops and sought to stop the auction of contracts to sell arrack. The news papers covered the anti-arrack movement that was spearheaded by the women for a year. But the prohibition imposed by the state in 1993 on arrack was withdrawn in 1994 as it wanted additional revenue generated by liquor sales. The experience, however, gave the women's groups in Andhra Pradesh new confidence and power to check the alcohol abuse by men in their families, and to prevent domestic violence by alcoholic husbands.

CONCLUSIONS

One of the social evils confronting the Indian society is the menace of 'dowry'. Dowry is an amount or consideration (be it in cash or in kind) paid to the groom by the bride's family for marriage. Social scientists consider dowry as a major reason for increasing domestic violence against women. Although the dowry was legally prohibited in India in 1961, it continues to be highly institutionalized. Dowry death is considered as one of the many categories of violence against women. The practice of dowry abuse is rising in India. There were more than 5,000 dowry death cases registered in India in 1996 and it increased to more than 6000 by 2005. The highest dowry deaths were recorded in Uttar Pradesh followed by Bihar, Madhya Pradesh and Andhra Pradesh. Some times bride's parents are also responsible for perpetuation of violence related to dowry because they accept the custom of dowry by their tacit approval. The dowry deaths are increasing in India, though some of the anti dowry movements done by women in India like All India Democratic Women's Associations, the All India Democratic Women's congress, Nari Atma Raksha Samity etc. The police, medical and legal systems, and the judiciary are involved in the preventive and remedial measures. The bride and groom and their respective families, along with women's organizations, play an important role. There is, however, a dire need for the training of involved professionals, as well as awareness building in various societal groups.

References

Agnes, Flavia (1992), "Protecting Women against Violence? Review of a Decade of Legislation on Violence against Women: 1980-1989", *Economic and Political Weekly,* 27 (17), WS 21-34.

Agnes, Flavia (1998), "Violence in the Family: Wife Beating", in Rehana Ghadially (ed.) Women in Indian Society-A Reader, Sage Publications, New Delhi.

Baxi, Mamta (2001), Violence for Equality: A Report on Nari Adalat, Gujarat, Tata Institute of Social Sciences, Mumbai.

Bhattacharya, R. (2004), Behind Closed Doors Domestic Violence in India, Sage Publications, New Delhi.

Diwan, P. and Diwan, P. (1995), Dowry and Protection to Married Women, Deep and Deep Publications, New Delhi.

Ellisberg, M., Heise, L. and Shrader, E. (1999), Researching Violence against Women: A Practical Guide for Research and Advocates, Centre for Health and Gender Equity, Washington D.C.

Jai Singh, I. (1995), "Violence against Women: The Indian Perspective" in J. Peters and A. Walpes (ed.) Women's Rights, Human Rights, Sage Publications, New Delhi.

Kelkar, Govind (1991), Violence against Women in India: Perspective and Strategies, Asian Institute of Technology, Bangkok.

Mira Seta (2001), Women and Development: The Indian Experience, Crime against Women", Sage Publications, New Delhi.

Nangia, J. N. (1985), Dowry, Pragati Publications, Meerut.

National Crime Record Bureau (2005), National Crime Record Bureau Report, New Delhi.

Poonacha, Veena and Divya Pandey (1999), Response to Domestic Violence in States of Karnataka and Gujarat, Research Centre for Women Studies, SNDT Women's University, Mumbai.

Prasad, Shally (1999), Medico-Legal Response to Violence against Women in India, Violence against Women, 5 (5) 478-506.

Sharma Vinay (2007), The Widest Social Malaise, Deep and Deep Publications, New Delhi.

Singh, I. P. (1990), Indian Women: The Captured Beings, Intellectual Publication, New Delhi.

Domestic Violence in India

Ataur Rahman* & Shekh Belal Ahmad**

The United Nations declaration on the elimination of violence against women states in its Preamble that violence against women in the product of the "unequal power relation" that characterize gender relations in all party of the world. Glass defines domestic violence as "anything that is experienced as fearful, controlling and threatening when used by those with power (invariably men) against those without power (mainly women and children) (Ravindram, 1991). Domestic violence is one of the few phenomena which cut across all the cultural, socio-economic, educational ethnic and religious barriers. This type of violence not only seems to increase even with rise in women's education but also prevails among the elite sections of the society. In a survey on violence against women in India, 94 per cent of the cases involved an offender who was a member of the family (Naved, 2004).

CAUSES

Interference of in-laws, property dispute, alcoholism, extra marital affairs, marital maladjustment, personality disorder, drug addiction, dowry, economic crisis and divorce-related issues are the main causes of domestic violence in India.

The old method of reducing tension seem to have become an inadequate or unsuitable; as a consequence many resort to alcoholism for relief this leads to family disorganization and violent behaviorism in the family. The evils of dowry and the role it plays in the abuse of women provide an additional dimension to domestic violence in India. Economic crises arise from several reasons. Such as unemployment indebtedness loss of sources of livelihood, destitution arising from natural calamities like floods, earthquakes and cyclones.

* *Guest Faculty, Women's College, AMU, Aligarh.*

** *Department of Sociology and Social Work, AMU, Aligarh*

KINDS OF DOMESTIC VIOLENCE

Domestic violence is of many kinds. It can take many forms and variation and it can happen once in a while or all at the same time. Domestic violence can be psychological abuse, social abuse financial abuse physical assault. Violence can be criminal and include physical assault or injury. It could be hitting, beating and shoving. It could be sexual abuse as well. It means forced sexual activity or stalking.

Right from the beginning the society conditions or rather train the female members to take care of house, their siblings their parents and so on and so forth. Whether they are working or not that is no consideration but are supposed to look after the kids and husband as well.

GENDER BIAS

Women's position in Indian society has been partly shaped by the ideology of the Indian family. Although the family is theoretically a sanctuary for women it also has the potential of acting as a prison with a restrictive code of conduct (Abraham, 1995). The hierarchy of relationship that typically characterize a patriarchal home, "develops along age and gender lines" (D'cruz and Bharat, 2001), so that young women entering a patriarchal household are vulnerable to acts of violence from their marital family. In fact various studies show that if new member of the household is unable to adjust to the household suffer with greater indignities and humiliation (Mukhopadhyay, 1988; Ghadially and Kumar, 1988). Also, when a woman does not succumb to traditional socialization and does not conform to traditional gender roles, she is more likely to be beaten by her family (Goode and Tambiah, 1973). These acts of violence also tend to be socially accepted (Agnes, 1990; Srinivasn, 1998).

DOWRY RELATED DEATHS

Dowry is the payment in cash or kind by the brides family to the bridegroom's family along with the giving away of the bride (called *kanyadan*) in Indian marriage. *Kanyadan* is an important part of Hindu marital rites. *Kanya* means daughter and *dan* means gift. Dowry originated in upper caste families as the wedding gift to the bride from her family. The dowry was later given to help with marriage expenses in the case that her in-laws mistreated her. Although the dowry was legally prohibited in 1961, it continues to be highly institutionalized. The groom often demands a dowry consisting of a large sum of money farm furniture and electronic goods and appliances.

Dowry deaths occur when the young women, unable to bear the harassment and torture commits suicide are by hanging or by fire. Sometimes the woman is killed by setting her on fire; this is known as "bride burning".

DOMESTIC VIOLENCE AND HUMAN RIGHTS:

Undoubtedly, domestic violence is a human rights issue and serious impediment to the development. The Viena accord of 1994, the Beijing declaration and the platform for action (1995) hence accepted this fact the protection of women from domestic violence Bill 2005 having been passed by the Lok Sabha on 24th August 2005 and by the Rajya Sabha 29th august 2005 received the assent of the president of Indian on 13th September, 2005 and came on the statute book as the protection of women from Domestic Violence Act, 2005.

The present act clearly scores over the former bill. Under section 3 of the 2005 act, domestic violence is defined in terms of mental, physical sexual verbal emotional and economic abuse. The extent of domestic violence extends from physical hurt to emotional and economic blackmail and may be interpreted by courts and lawyers to include and punish marital rape as well. The act introduces the concept of domestic relationship. This has broadened the scope of those who may ask for relief under the act. The present act requires only the proof of domestic relationship as the basis for action.

The second most important advance made by the act is to understand the nature of domestic violence has been in the combination of civil and criminal remedies. The relief system in the act clearly shows the attempt on the part of the legislature to the accused to have access to a variety of relief measures, to be adopted to different circumstances. The Domestic Violence Act provides monetary compensation protection orders and residence orders. A protection order is a relief measure that is used in most domestic violence legislation internationally. It is a method by which domestic violence is sought to be curbed by issuing directions to the offender.

CONCLUSION

Various researches regarding domestic violence have shown that nearly one-third of Indian women who experience domestic violence have thought about running away from that family but fear of leaving their young children and having nowhere any place to go stop them to do so. In such circumstance, community intervention could be proved helpful here, the role of media is very important. It could go a long way in helping to provide, it becomes more sensitive to women's rights. The government official responses also need to be made more sensitive and progressive to the cause of women's right.

It is the fundamental right of all Indian citizens to enjoy life and liberty and it is the duty of the state to ensure that they can do so within the framework provided by the constitution of Indian and the international obligations such as CEDAW which India has accepted.

Violence against women greatly affect the children in the family. There is a correlation between violence against women and child mortality. Children who witness violence in the family are at higher risk for a whole range of emotional and behavioral problems including anxiety, depression, poor school performance and low self-esteem. The children become more prone to commit crimes and offence.

Studies related to domestic violence from around the world points to the fact that violence against women can only be combated if there is a healthy partnership between women groups and the state apparatus. While women's groups must protect their independence on certain issues they have to work 'effectively with the criminal justice system, joining forces to protect the rights of the exploited and subjugated women.

References

Ahuja R. (1987), "Crimes against Women", Rawat Publications, Jaipur.

Coomaraswamy Radhika (2005), "Human Security and Gender Violence", *Economic and Political Weekly*, October 29, pp. 4729-4736.

Flavia Agnes (1990), "Journey to Justice", Majlis, Mumbai.

Flavia, Agnes (1992), "Protecting Women against Violence", *Economic and Political Weekly*, 25 April 1992.

Gonsalves Lina (2001), "Women and Human Rights, APH Publishing Corporation, New Delhi.

Jejeebhoy Shireen (1998), "Wife Beating in Rural India–A Husband's Right?", *Economic and Political Weekly*.

Karlekar M. (1998), "Domestic Violence", *Economic and Political Weekly*, 4 July.

Kornblit A. L. (1994), "Domestic Violence-an Emerging Health Issue", *Social Sciences and Medicine*, 39 (9).

Sehgal Rashme, "Delays do not Bode Well for Domestic Violence Bill", *www.infochangeindia.org*.

Sen Srijoni and Ambast, Sanhita, "The Domestic Violence Act, 2005: A New Direction", *www.indlaw.com*.

"The Protection of Women from Domestic Violence Act, 2005 (Bare Act), Universal Law Publishing Co. Pvt. Ltd., Delhi.

Index

V

W